RENT to RENT

GETTING STARTED GUIDE

JACQUIE EDWARDS

Rent to Rent - Getting Started Guide

First published in 2017 by

Panoma Press Ltd
48 St Vincent Drive, St Albans, Herts, AL1 5SJ, UK
info@panomapress.com
www.panomapress.com

Book layout by Neil Coe.

Printed on acid-free paper from managed forests.

ISBN 978-1-784521-06-6

The right of Jacquie Edwards to be identified as the author of this work has been asserted in accordance with sections 77 and 78 of the Copyright, Designs and Patents Act 1988.

A CIP catalogue record for this book is available from the British Library.

This book is available online and in bookstores.

FOREWORD

When I started out on my mission to build a map of wealth creation, I was buried in information and had no clear path that I thought would work for me. I took the usual approach of trial and error and what I realised on my journey is that you don't need just *information*, you need **direction**. Information is like a map of an area, it is all the detail of **everything**, but you don't know where you are, or even maybe where you need to get to. **Direction** comes from your GPS, where you know where you're starting, plug in where you want to be and it gives you a few routes to get there.

I have been working with Jacquie over the last few years and followed her progress closely. We have talked a lot about making impactful businesses and so when she asked me, "How could I impact more investors?" I said, "Well, you have shared the strategy with them, why not put together a book with some direction for them?" and here it is! Her first best-seller focused on the Rent to Rent strategy, this one gives you **direction** on how to chart a safe course from starting up, to scaling a successful property investing business. These steps are tried and tested, following the eight stages of enterprise growth.

In my late twenties I was running a start-up property investment magazine. I got to meet and interview a lot of property investors who had all sorts of different experience. They all said that they believed property investing was the key to creating long-term wealth (…well they would!). My favourite question to ask in the interview was, "What was the most challenging part in your journey?" and they almost always answered, "Knowing the next steps to take when you are outside of your comfort zone." The key thing I have learnt is that you don't need to know all of the steps, just the next one to take right now.

When you are just starting out in any new venture, the amount of things to do can seem overwhelming. Jacquie has broken down everything that needs to be done into a few key areas: planning your business, keeping it legal, researching your goldmine area, setting up your marketing machine, presenting your offer and next steps to grow your business. This book will help to build your confidence, avoid some of the pitfalls and help you to get results more quickly by following a proven model.

So I'll leave you with one more thought. I often get asked, "Roger, when is the best time to start investing?" and my answer is always the same, "You are in luck because there are only two best times. The first best time is twenty years ago…" "Hmm, well I can't do that, so when is the second best time?" "The second best time is **NOW**." Are you ready to set your GPS and take the first step?

Keep making magic.

Roger James Hamilton

Author of New York Times Bestseller *Millionaire Master Plan*. Founder of Entrepreneurs Institute.

CONTENTS

STEP 3: RESEARCH YOUR AREA   105

STEP 4: DO A LOT OF VIEWINGS   **133**

STEP 5: NEXT STEPS/SCALING   **161**

INTRODUCTION & WELCOME

Hello and thank you for letting me join you on your property journey! I am truly excited to help you get started with your Rent to Rent business. I've got loads of experience working on my own Rent to Rent business and helping many others to create successful businesses as well.

You may have read my first book, *Rent to Rent: Your Questions Answered.* But don't worry if you haven't read that one as I would consider this book a prequel to that. *Your Questions Answered* was based on my coaching and mentoring experience and the main questions people were asking me when they were trying to get their Rent to Rent business up and running. It is a Q&A style book that answers specific questions such as: What contracts should I use? How do I know how much rent to charge? How do I find prospective deals? etc. That book has loads of really useful information as a reference book to use when you are working and in the midst of things. It's had amazing reviews and was a No.1 bestseller on Amazon and I consistently meet people who have had great results because of the book. But I was still getting calls and emails from people who just weren't quite able to get started. Who needed just a little bit more to really help them accelerate their journey. It took me a while to understand what that little bit extra might be because all of the knowledge is in the *Your Questions Answered* book – it has all the information and answers all the key questions to getting your business up and running and how to manage it going forward. So I didn't know what was missing.

Then one day I had someone call for one of my FREE 10-minute coaching calls and she asked if I had a checklist of what she needed to do to get started. And that's when the proverbial lightbulb went on in my head. While I put all of the information in *Your Questions Answered* and it follows the process from beginning to end, it isn't as structured as a checklist. That book will give you all the answers to your questions but won't tell you which bits you need to do first, second and third in order to practically get your business up and running. And it won't help you make sure you have done all the steps, so without this checklist there is always a chance you will miss a step. That is when this book, *Rent to Rent: Getting Started Guide* was born. I absolutely love a checklist and this is a true hands-on practical guide to make sure you get your Rent to Rent business set up correctly.

This book is your guide to getting started and setting up a successful business. It goes through each step in detail that I used to set up my Rent to Rent business and what my students have used to set up their businesses. It is filled with loads of practical hands-on application material like checklists and templates. One of my core skills is in organising information and systemising businesses; this book really is a practical guide that will help you focus on and set up your Rent to Rent business in a very orderly manner so that it will be easy to scale and shape the business to be exactly what you want it to be as it grows. You will be able to follow along step by step to get your own business organised, starting with Step 1 – planning, through to how to do the viewings to find the first property. Because this is the *getting started guide* we will stop at the place where you get the property as that's the point where you can transfer over to the *Rent to Rent: Your Questions Answered* book to get tips on managing the tenants and I've provided some other useful next steps material as well.

WHO THIS GUIDE IS FOR

I bet you want to know if this book is right for you. If you are like me, you want to get all the facts and get your business up and running and making you money as quickly as possible! There are a couple of different types of people that I've written this book specifically for:

1. You are brand new to Rent to Rent. Maybe you heard me (or someone else) speak at an event about Rent to Rent or maybe you've just stumbled across Rent to Rent when looking for a way to get into property when you don't have enough for a huge deposit. No matter how you found out about Rent to Rent, if you are brand new this book is perfect for you because it will take you step by step through exactly what you need to do to get started.

2. You have been working on Rent to Rent for a while but feel a bit overwhelmed and maybe a bit lost. If this is you, you may have taken a course or two and have implemented some of the actions but still feel that something is missing. You are worried you forgot an important piece of the puzzle but don't know how to find out which piece is missing. This book is perfect for you because you can see

the exact steps in order and you can tick off the ones that you've done and narrow down to any that you have missed so that you can quickly implement them to complete your business.

3. You already have a property business or a few properties that you own and are looking to increase cash flow by adding the Rent to Rent strategy. If this is you then you are in a great place. With the experience of having your own properties behind you, you've got a lot more credibility in the business than those people starting with no experience. But you've also got some preconceived notions that might be holding you back as well. And Rent to Rent is different from just going out and buying properties as there are some things you need to do when managing other people's properties that you don't need to worry about when managing your own. So this book will highlight those differences and help you incorporate all of your properties into one cash-flowing property machine!

4. You really loved my other book, *Rent to Rent: Your Questions Answered* and just wanted to read this book as you knew it would be awesome too. First, thank you so much for supporting me! And second, welcome back! Hopefully you are taking amazing action from the first book and have been following my blog and other material on both my personal and Rent to Rent websites and so you are moving forward at speed with your Rent to Rent business. If you've read all the material and still haven't managed to put it all together, this book will be

perfect as it will give you the step by step start-up so you can make sure you are doing all the steps in the right order. And if you have already started and even have a few properties, then well done! This book will be a refresher for you. Sometimes, as we advance in our businesses, it is good to have a back to basics session to make sure you still have those key fundamentals in place.

If you don't fit into one of the categories above, don't worry. There is always information to be gleaned from any book. I've got loads of good solid foundation material that can be used in any business – not just in your Rent to Rent business. What sets me apart from many property investors is my business experience and knowledge. I spent many years as an accountant working with some massive global businesses and helping them keep their processes organised and auditable, so I'm the perfect person to help you keep things (or get things) organised in yours! I love checklists, flowcharts and processes and I have included quite a few of them in this book.

HOW TO USE THIS BOOK

This book is structured as a step by step guide. My other book, *Rent to Rent: Your Questions Answered*, was designed as a dip in and dip out Q&A style book. This one is similar as you don't have to start at the very beginning and where you start can depend on where you are at in your journey. However, I would strongly suggest that you start at the beginning with Step 1 and go through the book in the order that it is presented. Even if you think you have already completed a step, I urge you to go through all the material in the book (and in the FREE downloadable resources) as there is always a chance that you can pick up a little golden nugget of information that will help tweak your business in ways that you weren't expecting.

If you are brand new to property and Rent to Rent, then you should definitely start at Step 1 and go through the full planning stage. In fact, I think everyone should go through the full planning stage as I've found that most people don't spend enough time planning their businesses and after all:

If you fail to plan, you are planning to fail.

Then for those that hate to follow the crowd and want to break free from the constraints of structure, once you've got through Step 1, where you have set your goals and created a firm action plan and budget, then you can move through the other steps as and when you'd like. Again, I have put them in the order they are in for a reason and if you are new to the business it's probably easiest to do everything in order. But if you've dabbled in property before or done some other trainings then you may already have some of the steps completed, and in that case you can jump around a bit. Do make sure that you don't miss any steps though as each one is important in its own way and all of them contributed to my ability to create the strong and profitable Rent to Rent business that I built. After all, why reinvent the wheel when I've done it all for you?

There is also an electronic component to this book. You don't have to use the Online Resources to get full value from this book but if you are able to they will add even more value to what is contained in here. The Online Resources contain downloads, templates and videos that I use in my own business along with a detailed checklist that follows the outline of this book that you can use to monitor your own progress (and is especially satisfying for those of you that really enjoy physically ticking off items from your to-do list). You can find those resources at the following website: www.R2RGuide.com. There will also be links to the Online Resources throughout the book.

WHO I AM

If this is your first time meeting me – Hello! I've got a Rent to Rent business that I started in 2014 with my partner, Anthony D'Souza. That business has grown now to 20 properties and over 100 tenants in the last two and a bit years. When I started the business I had no property experience. I didn't even own my own home, but I knew I needed a change so that I could get out of the rat race. I had spent the last 10 years as an accountant which felt like being a round peg in a square hole. I didn't fit in very well… to say the least! I worked for one of the largest accounting firms in the world and was lucky enough to get transferred from my home office (in the USA, where I'm from) to London but I was unlucky that it happened right at the time of the credit crunch. So all of the work had dried up for the specific team I worked for and the office got that nasty corporate back-stabbing vibe. So I started to look for something else.

The only thing I thought I could do was accounting because, after all, hadn't I spent four years in university studying accounting and five years at that point working on a career in it? I had to stick with accounting or my university degree would be a waste of money, right?

So I left the firm and went to work at a large corporation in their accounting department. This was much, much better – a much friendlier atmosphere – but I was still an accountant. I kept looking forward and thinking is *this* what I am going to be doing for the next 40 years of my life? I'm sure many people have felt the same thing.

From there I jumped to freelance accounting. I thought being self-employed would change everything. I envisioned days and weeks of working from home in my PJs with the ideal of picking my own clients so that I could work six months and travel six months. This was the true ideal for me. But sadly, as an accountant my clients expected me to be in their offices when I was working and it was basically just like any normal job except I got to move around a bit more and I was able to do a lot more travelling. But I was still an accountant and not enjoying life to the full that I thought was possible.

So I started reading books to see what else was out there. The first two that stood out for me were *The Four Hour Workweek* by Tim Ferriss and *Rich Dad, Poor Dad,* by Robert Kiosaki. These started putting a lot more entrepreneurial ideas in my head. Ideas outside the realm of just staying as an accountant. So I started to look a bit further afield for ideas on how to build the future and the financial freedom I wanted.

I started dabbling a bit in things like FX trading, network marketing and things like that. Again, I'm sure there are others out there that have been looking around to find another, better way than just the normal 9-5 job (or Just Over Broke as I've heard it called). I didn't want to be someone that worked the 40-40-40 (40 hours a week for 40 years to retire with 40% of the income) and I know you don't either! But FX trading wasn't my thing as the strategy that I learnt involved trading every single day from about 6.30am to 10.00pm and constantly watching the markets. Honestly, it was a bit beyond me and I didn't want something that I had to do every day! Then the network marketing I thought was amazing! It was a great concept and I started out really excited, but the way I learnt how to do it involved a lot of getting out and talking to people, which was a real struggle for me as I'm very much an introvert and networking is not one of my favourite or core skills. So I soon realised that this specific model wasn't for me.

That's when I really started to look into property investing. It features highly in *Rich Dad, Poor Dad* along with being highly recommended by a lot of other very rich and successful people.

Before I start anything I like to get educated about it. I had taken numerous training courses on FX trading and network marketing, not to mention the years I spent studying accounting before that. So I am a firm believer in truly spending time learning and understanding your field before jumping in. And property investing is no different. First, I started by reading books like Simon Zutshi's *Property Magic* which gave me a great overview of the UK property market and the different strategies that were possible. Up until then I thought you could just buy a property to rent it out or buy a property to refurbish it and flip it. But by reading a few books and attending some pin (Property Investors' Network) meetings I began to realise that there is a whole world of different strategies available for investing in property. It was early 2013 when I started really looking into property investing. I remember it was January that I went to my first PIN meeting. I was terrified because I hated going to networking events, but I made it through the evening and I learnt loads (although I'm pretty sure I didn't talk to anyone and ran out as soon as I could because I was so nervous that someone might try to talk to me). But I kept going back and I kept learning more each month. And I finally started talking to people. In July that year I attended a three-day property training course and even managed to bring along my partner (as he wasn't too interested in property before then; in fact, he only came on the course with me to make sure I didn't buy any more courses). We both loved the course and jumped into signing up for the 12-month programme that was starting the following January (2014). At this point I figured I had six months to get some experience and get some properties before we started the course as we wanted to have a bit of experience before we got started. And after all, hadn't I just spent three days learning all the strategies? I could surely get a few properties under my belt in the next six months.

So we started putting in place everything we learnt in the course. I did leaflets, postcards in shop windows, visited loads of estate agents and was travelling anywhere within two hours of my house to look at anything from one-bedroom flats to 20-bed B&Bs. After a few months I realised I couldn't focus on both my day job (I was still doing accounting freelance at the time) and property. So I had to make a decision and I decided to drop down to part-time at work and then after a few more months I dropped the accounting job altogether to give myself 12 months to make this 'property thing' work. (Note: this isn't something I recommend for most people – you need to evaluate your circumstances as quitting your job is quite a big deal.)

The results of six months of running around chasing the property investor dream was that just before my 12-month course started we still had ZERO properties! I was tired and stressed and disillusioned. I had a chat with my coach and told him that I didn't think this property thing was going to work and I was ready to give up. Luckily, my coach wasn't ready for me to give up. He saw me going through what almost every other new property investor goes through in the chasing of shiny pennies. I was trying to do every strategy with no focus and no plan. And luckily he caught me before I gave up and had a serious chat with me about what I was doing and why I was doing it. And that was when I realised that just knowing all the different property strategies wasn't the same thing as having a real plan and being a property investor. I needed to sit down and treat my property investing like a business and put together a business plan and focus on one strategy in one area.

That's when I chose Rent to Rent. After reviewing what my goals were (fast cash flow so I could leave my job) I went through the key strategies that would get me there. For me at the time the main cash flow strategy was using HMOs (houses of multiple occupation). So I started looking at HMO opportunities in my area, which is Oxford. Now, Oxford is very expensive; it is said to be the most expensive city in the country to buy houses based on income, which means it's more expensive than London because people get paid less than in London, basically. Because of this it is really difficult to find an HMO that 'stacks'. Also, Oxford has Article 4 and additional licensing in place regarding HMOs, which means locally that any property with three or more unrelated people sharing needs to have planning permission from the council and a licence from the council. This makes it very difficult to create new HMOs and therefore increases the price of properties that are already HMOs. Of course it is still totally possible to find great HMO deals to purchase that cash flow well and have a great return on investment, but they are a bit fewer and farther between. And in general I was also seeing most properties that would need about £100,000 deposit just to purchase the property. That meant if we were able to get a mortgage (which again is very tough for a first-time buyer to get an HMO mortgage) we would need to have £100,000 deposit, which would take all our cash and we wouldn't have anything left. And while one HMO could make £500-1,000 per month cash flow, that wasn't enough to let me quit my job. So I needed a strategy that would allow me to get multiple HMOs all bringing me £500+ profit per month, with low start-up capital and no mortgage. That lines up perfectly with the Rent to Rent strategy and it all started from there.

My Year 1 target was £100,000 profit from Rent to Rents with a focus on HMOs in Oxford. With a lot of hard work and mostly with a lot of taking action I smashed that target in the first year and have gone on to nearly double it after that. There were some mistakes and some tears along the way and a lot of uncertainty about the process and if I was going about everything correctly. Luckily, today I've got a great business and am financially free through the Rent to Rent strategy and I'm able to help other people achieve that goal as well. This guide is born of my work in that first year getting everything set up properly and treating my property investing as a business. Because of my business background and with the help of my coach in identifying (and reminding me of) my business skills set, I was able to use a systemised approach with my business from the very beginning and I'm going to share that system with you in this step by step guide. It helped me to build my life-changing Rent to Rent business and if you follow the guide and take action it can help you with yours as well!

ADDITIONAL RESOURCES THROUGHOUT THE BOOK

In this age of the internet I've decided to make use of it to easily list out the additional resources that will be mentioned throughout the book. I've created a completely FREE module on the Rent to Rent Academy website just for YOU with all the resources and a few extra bonuses related to this book. You can find it here: www.R2RGuide.com

This module will contain some step by step videos going through some of the processes throughout the book, along with downloads of some of the files and templates that we use in our Rent to Rent business. I hope that just because the resources are free you won't ignore them, as I know a lot of people don't value what comes free. I have put just as much effort into the creation and listing of the resources as I have into the writing of this guide and the two go hand in hand together. I'm a firm believer in not reinventing the wheel when you get started on your business so I've shared a load of content and created some downloads so that you can get started quickly using the same resources I used to build my successful Rent to Rent business.

Check out the FREE Resources at www.R2RGuide.com

THE STEPS

There are four main steps to getting started with Rent to Rent:

1. Plan Your Business

2. Set Up Your Business

3. Research Your Area

4. Do a Lot of Viewings

I've also added a fifth step at the end that will give you some ideas on your next steps once you've got your business up and running and have your first few properties under your belt, as I don't want to leave you hanging when you are ready to start scaling the business.

Now, first things first – in order to get started you need a lot more than just the four high-level steps. So each of those steps breaks down into a number of smaller objectives that will build upon each other to help you grow your Rent to Rent business. I've put the full checklist with all the steps and objectives into a downloadable checklist that you can use to track your progress as you proceed through the guide. You can find the downloadable version in the Online Resources at www.R2RGuide.com. And for completeness of the book I've listed all the steps below and we will go through each one in detail in the following sections of this guide.

1. Plan Your Business

    a.   Set Annual Goals

    b.   Plan Your Business

    c.   Establish Your Budget

    d.   Determine Your Rental Model

2. Set Up Your Business

    a.   Understand the Legal Requirements

    b.   Create a Professional Image

3. Research Your Area

    a.   Test Tenant Demand

    b.   Understand Local Prices

    c.   Get to Know the Competition

    d.   Estimate Your Bills

    e.   Become Familiar with National and Local Requirements

    f.   Running the Numbers

4. Do a Lot of Viewings

    a.   Set Up Your Marketing Machine

    b.   The Scripts to Get Started

    c.   Viewing Checklist

    d.   Presenting Your Offer

5. Next Steps/Scaling Your Business

THE BREAKDOWN

Now that you know the basic list and have your guide to getting started on your Rent to Rent journey, let's break each step down into bite-sized action plans. This section of the book will take you through each stage of the plan in greater detail. I suggest that you follow each step in the order that it is presented in the checklist. You may already have some pieces in place and I still recommend that you read through everything as there are always little golden nuggets that you can pick up in the most unexpected places. I've threaded a theme throughout the guide that is the true key to succeeding in this business. It's really important that you find the key yourself and interpret the meaning most relevant to you. I've scattered the hints and left little trails throughout the guide and it's up to you to follow the path to true success! I've seen so many people succeed and I know you can too by following this guide. Let's get started!

STEP 1:
PLAN YOUR BUSINESS

You need to start with a plan in any business – and your Rent to Rent business is no different. I see so many people skip this step. They think that by choosing Rent to Rent as their strategy then that is their plan. It's not! You need to put pen to paper and make a much more detailed plan. There is a quote I love:

> *A dream written down with a date becomes a goal.*
>
> *A goal broken down into steps becomes a plan.*
>
> *A plan backed by action makes your dreams come true.*

Greg S. Reid

So in this step we are going to convert your dreams into goals and plans which will be used to help steer your actions in the following steps so that you can start to make your dreams come true!

This step is also outlined in the online web resources and you can find additional downloadable material and videos to supplement your learning: www.R2RGuide.com.

1.1 Set Annual Goals

A dream written down with a date becomes a goal.

Every 1st January I used to sit down and set my New Year's resolutions (you know, those promises to yourself that never last). Actually, I used to do them on 31st December and think how great the next year was going to be. Then the next week I would be at the gym or eating my salads feeling all smug and healthy, but by February I was back in the same place as the previous year with my resolutions forgotten and my gym membership a distant memory.

Well, your business goals are pretty much the same thing as your New Year's resolutions and if you want to actually achieve your business goals and not have them go the way most New Year's resolutions go (i.e. forgotten), there are a few steps you need to take. I've read hundreds of business, goal-setting and personal development books and I've put together what I consider to be the best of all of them surrounding goal setting. The following information is basically my annual goal-setting system for success – I call it the *Rent to Rent Success System*! All of the information is here in this book and I have also included a downloadable version that you can follow and fill out step by step in the Online Resources (www.R2RGuide.com).

Business (and other!) projects have a natural flow that lends itself to a continual improvement cycle: Understand, Plan, Do and Review. This section will go step by step through each of these at a high level for your overall annual goals, then breaks those down into monthly, weekly and daily goals and tasks.

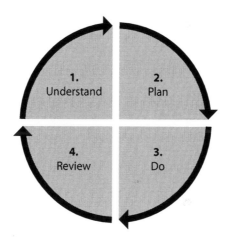

Step 1. Understand what you are trying to achieve, the problems and the objectives.

Step 2. Plan the best approach

Step 3. Do the implementation and perform the task.

Step 4. Review the results and look for improvements.

By following these four steps you will be setting yourself up for success. You will not only be deciding your actions based on your goals but you will be reviewing those actions to ensure you are moving forward in the best possible manner and correcting for any errors or changes along the way.

1.1.1 Step 1 – Understand

Understand what you are trying to achieve, the problems and the objectives.

This first step of the *Rent to Rent Success System* is really broken down into two parts:

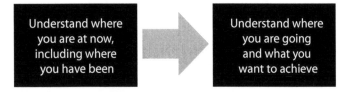

In order to know where you want to go and how to get there you need to know where you are. It's like using the satellite navigation system for your car. The system needs to know where you are starting from in order to plan the best route. First we are going to take a moment now to understand where you are coming from in your business and your life.

To understand where you are coming from and what you have accomplished and learnt in the last 12 months this system has a series of questions for you to answer. These questions are personal and will help you to understand the past 12 months and what has worked and what hasn't worked. It's important to both celebrate the achievement and accomplishments of the past and also to learn from the mistakes and failures so that you don't repeat them. By taking the time to understand where you have come from it will be easier to understand where you are at now.

Exercise: Understanding the Past 12 Months

- What are your top three achievements from the past 12 months?

- What are the top three lessons you learnt in the past 12 months?

- What are the top three personal improvements you made in the last 12 months?

- What are the top three things you would go back and do differently?

- What are your top five important events from the past 12 months?

- What are the top three things you are most grateful for in the past 12 months?

- Who are your top three relationships from the past 12 months?

- What is the top word that best describes your past 12 months?

- What was the best decision you made in the past 12 months?

- What was the worst decision you made in the past 12 months?

- What was the biggest risk you took in the past 12 months?

- What are the three things you need to do more of in the next 12 months?

- What are the three things you need to do less of in the next 12 months?

- What are the three things you need to stop doing?

Next it's time to use what has happened in the past 12 months to understand where we are at now. To do this we will use The Wheel of Life. If you have been involved in coaching or personal development, you may have seen The Wheel of Life before as it is a common tool. But just because you may have seen it before, do not discount the power of its simplicity. This is a tool we will use regularly in the *Rent to Rent Success System*.

There are many different formats and categories for The Wheel of Life. We will use a modified one specifically for business as that is what this system is focused on. The categories and some questions to think about are as follows:

- **Business Plan:**

    - Do you have a written business plan?

    - Are you inspired by your business plan?

    - Are you committed to your business plan?

- **Financial Plan:**

    - Do you have a written budget and do you stick to your budget?

    - Do you have a cash flow forecast and know how you are funding the next six months?

    - Do you track your results and know how to minimise your taxes?

- **Sales and Marketing:**

    - Do you know who your customers are/will be and what they are looking for?

    - Do you have a sales funnel in place?

    - Do you know your conversion rates?

- **Networking:**

    - Do you attend networking meetings regularly?

    - Do you follow up with people that you have met while networking?

    - Do you know who you need to meet to further your business?

- **Systemising:**

    - Do you have a plan to take yourself out of the business?

    - Have you recorded processes and procedures?

    - Do you have regular reviews with your team?

- **Personal Development:**

  - Do you regularly read or listen to developmental books?

  - Are you consistently learning and improving your skills?

  - Are you involved in training and mentoring programmes?

- **Health:**

  - Do you make time for exercise on a weekly basis?

  - Do you eat nutritious meals?

  - Do you get eight hours sleep per night?

- **Lifestyle**

  - Do you have hobbies outside of work?

  - Do you know when your next holiday is?

  - Do you regularly spend time with friends and family?

Exercise: Understanding the Present

Using the previous questions as guides, mark on a scale of 1-10 (1 being the lowest and 10 being the highest) how satisfied you are with each area of your business. Then connect the marks to create a diagram that will highlight areas you may need to focus on in the upcoming 12 months (see example). I suggest that you repeat this process monthly throughout the year so that you can measure your progress. And remember that if you head to the Online Resources (www.R2RGuide.com) and check out the *Rent to Rent Success Plan*, there is a copy of this in there for you to write on.

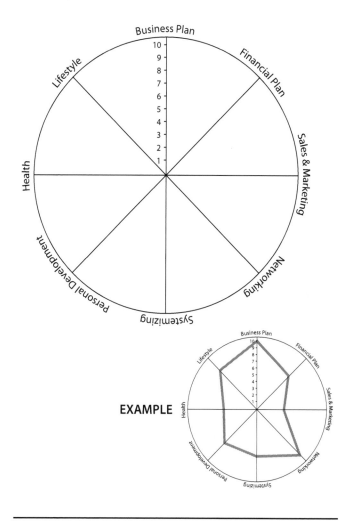

The last step of this section is understanding what you want to achieve in the next 12 months. We've discovered where we are coming from and where we are at now so one last thing to programme into the navigation system is where do you want to go? The *Rent to Rent Success System* will take you through a process of breaking down your big annual banner goals into smaller bite-sized chunks to help you tackle them in a timely and productive manner.

This can be pictured as an upside-down triangle, with the big annual goal at the top in the largest part of the triangle and then broken down into smaller, bite-sized goals for the months and weeks as you move to the smaller point of the triangle. This is something that you should be filling out on a weekly basis throughout the year.

But first we need to discover what our annual goal is. And that's right – goal is singular. We are going to really FOCUS (Follow One Course Until Successful) over the next 12 months. By focusing on just one thing and really going for it you will be a lot more likely to succeed than if you take a scattergun approach and try to achieve multiple goals (watch out for those shiny pennies).

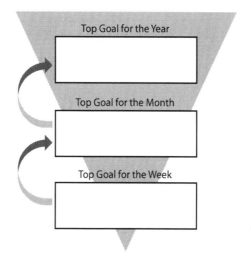

Exercise: Understanding Your Goal

Let's do some brainstorming to find out what the most important goal is for you.

First – make a list

I've added a list of areas that you will want to think about for your life and some examples of goals that you might want to set. Hopefully at the end of this exercise you will have 5-10 goals in each section, maybe even more!

This is one of the most important steps in the entire annual planning process. Don't filter yourself during this initial brainstorming. Just let everything come out and we will narrow it down in the following steps.

Make sure you write everything down that you want to accomplish this year. Take your time with this exercise as finding the right goal is what can make or break your business. If you spend the next 12 months working towards the wrong goal your business is unlikely to flourish.

- **Business Goals**

    - Examples: market position, strategy, number of Rent to Rents, branding, team growth, improved performance, etc.

- **Financial Goals**

    - Examples: revenue growth, profit targets, savings/investment goals, asset value, pension planning, etc.

- **Sales & Marketing Goals**

    - Examples: product development, marketing targets, sales goals, conversion tracking, lead generation, etc.

- **Networking Goals**

    - Examples: types of contacts, number of events, contact conversions, contact links, etc.

- **Systemising Goals**

    - Examples: team development, system development, personal hours worked, recorded processes, etc.

- **Personal Development Goals**

    - Examples: books read, courses attended, skills learnt, finding a mentor, improved personal performance, etc.

- **Health Goals**

    - Examples: ideal weight, competitive events (marathon, 10k, etc.) reduce cholesterol, meditation, hours of sleep, nutrition, etc.

- **Lifestyle Goals**

    - Examples: time spent with family, holidays, partners, date night, attend children's events, shorter work weeks, relocating, volunteering, religion, mentoring others, etc.

Second – narrow it down (top 10)

Now that you've done the brainstorming and come up with lots of different goals and accomplishments, it is time to start narrowing it down by choosing your Top Ten Goals. These are the goals that really struck you while you were brainstorming. The ones that made your heart skip or the butterflies in your tummy flutter. They might not always be the ones you expected so keep an open mind and write down the goals from above that struck you the most. Then put a due date next to them.

Third – narrow it down some more (top 3)

How do you choose just one of those to focus on? Read through your goals again. Put a star next to the ones that can work together. For instance, is one of your goals to increase profit and another goal to complete X number of projects? If the projects will lead to the increase in profit, then maybe you can combine them to be one goal. Or maybe you have a goal that talks about setting up a conversion tracking system and a goal for hiring two new team members. Is there a way to combine them? Will the team members be working on the system? Will the team members be tracking the conversions? Will you need two team members if you implement the system or maybe you will only need one? Do not combine goals that cannot be interrelated. For instance, if you want to publish a book on property investing and lose two stone, there isn't a lot relevant between those two goals that you can combine so that similar tasks can accomplish both, and if they are too dissimilar you will lose focus.

Rewrite any of your goals that allow you to combine two or more goals that work together and limit to your top three goals.

Fourth – pick your top goal

Do you feel the magic starting to happen? Are the lightbulbs coming on and has the weight been lifted from your chest? Are these starting to look like goals you can achieve? We've still got to narrow your goals from the top three to the ONE goal that you will focus on for the year.

First, please make sure your top three goals are SMART (Specific, Measurable, Achievable, Relevant, Time-bound). If your goals meet all of these characteristics and can answer all of the following questions, you can proceed. If not, try rewording your goals until you get at least one that meets all of the SMART characteristics.

Specific = Be very clear about exactly what you want to accomplish.

Measurable = How will you demonstrate achievement? How will you know when you have achieved the goal?

Achievable = The goal should stretch you and still be attainable in your desired timeframe. Do you know someone else that has achieved something similar? Also, do you have control over the outcome?

Relevant = Is it applicable to where you are at and where you want to be? Is it aligned to your values?

Time-bound = Is there a timeframe and due date for completion?

List your ONE goal below that is SMART. Be brave, dream big and reach for the stars! If you still had more than one goal, this is the time to narrow it down and pick a focus. Choose the goal that speaks loudest to you by reading the goals aloud and choosing the one that resonates with you and your values.

I suggest you write this in the first person as if you have already achieved it. So if your goal is to take on five Rent to Rents and earn £50,000 per annum, the goal should be written as: I have five high cash flowing Rent to Rents that are bringing me a net profit of £50,000. This starts telling your brain that you have achieved this so it will work on making it happen.

It doesn't end with setting our goals. We are only just beginning. Now that we know what your ONE goal for the year is and we have a focus it's time to determine who you need to be to reach that goal. We will move on to the next phase of the system: Planning. Don't skip the planning phase because I'm sure there are all kinds of tasks you can set yourself and things you can do, but the number one thing that will help you succeed is changing yourself rather than changing the world to make it give you your goal. Achieving your goal is about knowing who you are and who you need to become. Because as you change and improve yourself, you will automatically move closer to the achievement of your goals!

1.1.2 Step 2 – Plan

Create a plan to achieve your goal

Now that you understand where you have been, where you are currently at and what you want to achieve, we are ready to move forward to the next step – planning. This is where we will start to determine who you need to become in order to achieve your goals and what your days and weeks need to look like.

We will have an overview planning session for the year here but the planning doesn't end with an annual review. It is something you should continue monthly, weekly, and even daily. And each plan should build to the broader plan above it and link to your goal.

As part of this *Rent to Rent Success Plan* you will have weekly planning and review sessions. We will cover how to perform those a bit later. For now, let's go through the high-level annual planning session. As we ended the previous step by discovering our ONE goal for the year, we will now determine who we need to be to achieve it.

Exercise: Planning Who You Need to Become

Let's discover the behaviours and habits that you need to start, stop and continue in order to become the person you need to be to achieve your goals. List at least three habits or behaviours for each category below:

- New habits and behaviours I need to START

- Old habits and behaviours I need to STOP

- Good habits and behaviours I need to CONTINUE

Now that you know what you need to do and stop doing, how are you going to implement that into your daily routine? How are you going to turn the positives into good habits that you can use to grow yourself towards your goal?

Exercise: Plan How You Can Implement the New Habits and Behaviours into Each Day

Write down the three habits that you will implement into your life on a regular basis to ensure that you become the person you need to be to meet your goal. For example, if your goal was to complete eight Rent to Rent projects in the next 12 months then maybe one of the habits that you will implement into your life is contacting potential investors on a monthly basis and keeping them informed of new projects and developments while understanding their investment needs and requirements.

Exercise: Plan Your Perfect Day

What will your perfect day look like now that you have implemented all these new habits and behaviours? Let's fast forward and look ahead to your ideal day in 12 months' time. What will you be doing? Where will you be doing it from? Who will you be doing it with? Write down your plan for what your life will look like in 12 months. And remember to write it as if you have already accomplished it. For example: I am so excited to be able to spend each morning with my partner meditating and then going for a walk through the countryside near our home. I am then able to spend the morning writing my newest book that will help thousands of people achieve the same results that I have and change their lives forever.

You can write this however you like. Some people like to create mind maps, some people like to create schedules, some people simply like to write it out in long form. Do whatever helps you to visualise and cement your Perfect Day in your mind.

1.1.3 Steps 3 & 4 – Do & Review

Putting it all Together

Is it all starting to come together? Now that you know what needs to happen, what you want to happen and who you need to become to get there, the next step is actually getting out there and doing it! This means breaking it down to a smaller more manageable weekly basis. We are not going to go into loads of detail on this because we will be focusing on the doing in the later sections of this book. But as we are talking about planning and going through the *Rent to Rent Success Plan* this is a good place to point out that the downloadable *Success Plan* contained in the Online Resources (www.R2RGuide.com) continues on and provides guides for weekly planning and review based on all of the information you just worked through.

Each week contains the full Understand, Plan, Do and Review cycle – although most of the doing is done outside of the book when you get out and take action on your plan! By continuing a weekly cycle like this you make sure you stay focused so that your goals don't go the way of New Year's resolutions and you will keep on target to achieving them! So make sure you log into the Online Resources (www.R2RGuide.com) and grab your free downloads for the full *Rent to Rent Success Plan*.

1.2 Plan Your Business

A goal broken down into steps becomes a plan.

We spent the last section setting your goals and providing you with the tools you need to set good goals and keep focused on them. Now we need to break those goals down into steps to turn them into a business plan.

My aim in this section is not to help you create a giant document that you will write once and never look at again. Like the kind of business plan a bank or lender would want to see. I want to help you create a real and usable document that will flow and grow with your business because let's be honest, your business will change over the next months and years. You will have new ideas and new opportunities will present themselves to you. It's so amazing what starts to happen once you open yourself to the possibilities. When I first got started and decided to move into property investing I never dreamt of where it would take me. Our first business plan didn't contain most of what we are doing in our business today. As we have progressed in our Rent to Rent business and spent time meeting new people and educating ourselves, we have been presented with so many more opportunities that would never have been possible when I was just an accountant working my 9-5 sitting in someone else's office. So with the business plans we are going to create here I want them to be useful documents that are able to capture key ideas and set you on the right path, but will allow for flexibility as you grow and won't overwhelm you to come back and keep them updated.

I call this the two-page business plan. You basically write it out on two pages of A4 paper. And yes, there is a download available for you in the Online Resources (www.R2RGuide. com) – so head over and check it out. Otherwise, grab your own piece of paper or electronic file and let's get started!

Exercise: The Two-Page Business Plan

Stage 1 - Big fat hairy goals and your reason WHY!

On the top half of the first side of your paper you should capture the reason WHY you are in business. Your why is what inspires others to work with you.

Below your reason why, add your goals, objectives and aspirations. This is your big goal that we uncovered in the last section. Written as a SMART goal (Specific, Measurable, Achievable, Relevant, Time-bound) followed by a breakdown of what makes up that goal. We've got a bit more space in this section to really dig in and explain the goal and make it super specific and uncover any of the smaller supporting goals.

Things that might go in this section:

- Financial goals: portfolio value, cash flow income, capital income, total revenue, total profit

- Number and type of properties to achieve the above and by when

- What products or services you will be offering

- Any non-financial goals you may have: knowledge, skills, systems, or contacts you might want to build

Stage 2 - Your strategies and market

On the bottom half of the first side of your piece of paper you should capture your strategies and markets: What are you going to do and where? Why are you convinced this is a good idea and that it will work? What timeframe are you committing to in order to make it happen to ensure you give it a fair run?

One of the key pieces of advice I have received and follow is that you should pick a path (carefully!) and stick to it until you make it work. A good suggestion has been to plan 80% of your time on your primary strategy, 15% on your secondary strategy and 5% on your tertiary strategy. Where possible, your strategies should flow into one another so that if an opportunity doesn't fit into the primary strategy then there is a high probability that it could be used in the secondary or tertiary strategy.

Strategy examples

- 80% – HMO with workers and young professional tenants

- 15% – LHA - where HMO licences are not available, or properties not suitable

- 5% – selling deals to other investors as part of a deal sourcing service

Pick the markets in which you wish to operate and why you believe these will work. What is the potential and size of opportunity? What is the competition doing? What products or services will you be offering? etc.

Once you have the strategy it is good practice to create a basic budget of income by product and strategy type and also expected costs for the business. This will allow you to get an idea of your cash flow and projected profit for the next few years. This will be invaluable if you are looking to obtain any loans from the bank or other investors as they will want to know what you expect to achieve to value your business to confirm how much they may be willing to invest/loan. In addition, it gives you a target to work to and measure your progress. We will cover budgeting in the next section of this book; I wanted to pull it out separately as it is so important and is a major place I see people struggle that are just getting started. But don't worry, I'll bring back some of my old accounting tools to help you break it down and keep budgeting really simple.

Stage 3 - Lead generation, advertising and marketing

Put together a basic marketing strategy in this section on the second side of your A4 piece of paper. Ask yourself the following questions:

- What is your plan for lead generation and follow up?

- What types of advertising and marketing campaigns are you planning to use? How much will they cost? What sort of conversion rates are you expecting to get? What type of market will you be targeting?

Remember, the narrower you target, the more likely you are to get quality leads, but are more likely to get fewer of them.

- How many campaigns of each type will you run? Consider the theory on at least five points of contact for someone to start to become familiar with you and your brand.

- What are the different types of campaigns you might want to run to attract motivated sellers, investors and tenants?

- Add your advertising costs into your top-level finance projections.

- How are you going to build your brand? What are the core values of your business and how are you going to get these across?

- What does your business look like to the outside world: marketing collateral, website, letterheads etc.?

Stage 4 - Delivery, management, people and systems

Once you get someone saying yes to your product (i.e. Rent to Rent) the real hard work starts and you need to get the works going and property tenanted as soon as possible. This is what you cover in the last section on your paper.

Consider how you are going to manage the delivery/ refurbishment phase. How much work are you planning to do on each property: where on the scale of light refurb to major development? What are the main steps and type of contractors you need to help you in line with your strategy above? How many different teams might you need based on the amount of work you are expecting? How long do the projects typically take? Are you going to manage them yourself, or have one of the contractors project manage them?

What referencing and check processes are you going to use to ensure you get good quality tenants into the property who will take care of it and pay their rent on time?

What are you going to do when things go wrong in the property and need to be sorted out? Will you be managing them yourself, or outsourcing that to someone else?

Who might you need to help you – what will your team look like? Consider what you are best at and weakest at. Focus on your strengths and building your team around you to account for your weaker areas.

How will you measure your performance and improve? What systems will you use in your business? To start with these should be really basic – you should be focusing on property, not building the perfect business systems! In any case, it is always good to try everything yourself for the first, second or third time to get a feel for how long it typically takes and how much it typically costs. After that you want to (or have someone who can help you to) think about how to eliminate, automate or delegate that process.

And it's that simple. Well, maybe that isn't simple yet because we haven't really got into the meat of Rent to Rent and the strategy, which is what we will be doing in the rest of this book. So don't worry if your two-page business plan is still looking a little bit empty. Like I said, this is a flowing document and will change as your business changes and as you grow in understanding as well. For now, have an outline with some of your high-level ideas and your key goal at the top and make sure you keep coming back to this business plan as you finish each of the sections of this book so that you can fill in any additional ideas. By the end of the book you should have the business plan full and set out so that you are comfortable with where you are going in your Rent to Rent business and how you will achieve your goal!

And just remember – your plan is there to help keep you on track. That means that you don't just put it in the drawer with a big smile on your face for having just completed it. You need to put it somewhere you can see it and review it every day. If you are lacking in motivation, or unsure on what to do next, just read through it and pick something – you won't go wrong. You are the person driving your business, not anyone else.

It helps to set aside some formal time to review your progress at a high level against the plan. I recommend you do this at least once a month. Now as we aren't always honest with ourselves it can be a very rewarding exercise to review your plan with someone else. It is much easier to be honest with yourself and less easy to make excuses as to why things haven't happened, especially when you have a coach or mentor to keep you accountable.

It is important that you hold yourself to account and don't remove or change objectives because you think you might not quite make it. If something has materially changed in the markets or your situation then it is OK to change the plan, but you will be amazed at how your subconscious works to focus you towards your goals and help you achieve them. If you start telling yourself that you don't need to achieve, or cut your goals down, then guess what – you probably won't achieve them. Whereas if you are getting close to a deadline and you still have some way to go, your subconscious will be helping you in all ways it can, picking out opportunities, changing the way you communicate with people.

1.3 Establish Your Budget

We talked briefly about budgeting in the last section when you were putting your plan together. We are going to go into more detail about budgets in this section. I know a lot of people let out a big inward groan (or maybe even outward) as I know budgeting and finances are most people's least favourite topic. To be honest, I used to be an accountant and I hate doing this stuff too. But it is hugely important for your business, especially when you are just getting started, as it can be really easy to just spend, spend, spend and if you are not tracking that spend one day you could wake up and realise that all the money you were going to use on your first Rent to Rent deal has been used up by your advertising.

Everyone is going to be starting from a different place and with a different amount of money to invest into their business. Rent to Rent is a great property strategy for people with small start-up capital (compared to purchasing properties with 25% deposits) but you still need some money to get started. There are quite a few start-up costs that we will go through as part of getting your business started. Things like registering with the Information Commissioners Office, getting public liability insurance, and joining a redress scheme are all necessary parts of getting your business started and all have costs associated with them which need to be considered as part of your planning phase.

I'm going to provide you with a basic structure for a beginning budget. If you love spreadsheets and manipulating data, feel free to transform this into your own creation – just make sure you don't spend more time on the spreadsheet than on actually getting your business going. If you don't love spreadsheets, you can easily use mine as there is a downloadable version in the Online Resources (www.R2RGuide.com).

Let's talk about what we are going to use this budget for. Initially this budget is going to be for you to use to get an understanding of all the different costs that can be associated with this business. As we go through each section of the book I'll tell you a bit about any costs necessary to implementing that section. I suggest you put each cost into your budget to start with so you can see a full picture of the maximum costs associated with the business. So this would include costs for all the different types of advertising, even if you only plan on using one or two methods, and include costs for all the possible insurances even though you might only need public liability at the moment. Once you know the maximum costs and investment necessary it will be much easier for you to make an informed and educated decision on how best to run your business to fit in your budget.

Exercise: Overall Budget

To start with we need to discover your overall budget. This is the total amount you have available to invest into your business, the amount of money that is the absolute maximum you have to cover everything from the cost of this book through to the first month's rent of your first Rent to Rent deal.

Start by writing down any lump sum amount you have right now. If you have £5,000 sitting in the bank set aside just for your Rent to Rent business (not for any living expenses), that's the first amount to write down at the top of your budget page.

Again, this number will be different for everyone. Some will have a higher initial budget and some might not even have any money to start with. And that's OK. It just means you will have to focus on slightly different things to get started; no matter where you are starting from you need a budget.

The next number you will write down is any monthly amount you will be able to set aside to go towards your Rent to Rent business. This is for people who will be working or have other profit-generating activities producing additional funds that you don't need to cover your day to day living expenses. So if you can put aside £50 every month out of your salary, write that as the next line on your budget paper. You may want to add a sentence or two reminder of where that money is coming from as well.

Finally, you need to establish your emergency fund. This is an amount of money set aside in case things go wrong – and things always go wrong so you must have an emergency fund. This doesn't have to be all cash although I recommend you have some cash set aside for emergencies; it can include available credit card balances, friends and family that you can go to for business loans, etc. Make sure this is realistic, and if you don't have an emergency fund then I urge you to take out some of the money from your overall budget and put it into your emergency fund. To start with the fund doesn't have to be huge, again it will depend what you are personally comfortable with. And as you grow, this fund will need to get bigger so that it can cover any voids, large maintenance issues, etc. and it's easier as your business gets bigger as well. For us, we are able to easily negotiate a £10,000 overdraft with our bank and could make that larger if necessary. When you are just getting started you won't need anywhere near that much – you decide what is comfortable for you.

Remember to grab the downloadable spreadsheet in the Online Resources (www.R2RGuide.com).

Now that you know your overall budget and funds available to invest into your Rent to Rent business let's get a bit more into the detail of how we set up and track our budget compared to our ongoing expenses. I'm going to give you the breakdown and the way that I tracked our budget for our business when we were getting started. You may have some additional items you want to add into the budget and track, which is fine. I urge you to keep it as simple as possible so that it's easy to do as ideally you need to keep it updated on at least a monthly basis, and the easier it is, the more likely you are to keep it updated (and I'm speaking from experience here as someone who likes complicated spreadsheets but has learnt to tone it down for stuff like this).

Next, let's move on to actually setting up the budget and tracking expenses. I use seven general categories for expenses, each with more detailed line items associated. Here is the full list that I use:

1. Advertising Expenses

    a.   Business Cards

    b.   Direct Mailing

    c.   Leaflet Delivery

    d.   Networking Meetings

    e.   Newspaper Ad

    f.   Online Advertising

    g.   Other

    h.   Phone Answering Service

    i.   Postcards/Leaflets

    j.   SpareRoom Membership/Ads

    k.   Website – Domain Registration

    l.   Website – Set Up

2. General Business Expenses

    a.   Bank Charges

    b.   Business Insurance

    c.   Consumables

    d.   Contracts with Landlords

    e.   Courier Charges

    f.   Deposit Membership

    g.   ICO Registration

    h.   Local Phone Number

    i.   Mobile Phone Charges

    j.   NLA/RLA Membership

    k.   Office Internet

    l.   Other

    m.   Professional Email Address

    n.   Redress Scheme Membership

3. Professional Expenses

    a.   Accountant

    b.   Bookkeeper

    c.   Consultants

    d.   Other

    e.   Solicitor

    f.   Subcontractors

4. Salary

    a.   Director Salary

    b.   Other

5. Systems

    a.   Accounting/Bookkeeping Systems

    b.   CRM System/Management Systems

    c.   Other

6. Training Expenses (Personal Development)

    a.   Books, Magazines, Subscriptions

    b.   Ongoing Training

    c.   Other

7. Travel Expenses

    a.   Hotels

    b.   Meals

    c.   Other

    d.   Transport – including mileage

These are the basic categories that I use and you can modify them to best suit your business. Again, this is just an overview section for budgeting and I don't expect you to know your exact budget right now. But by the end of the book you should be able to establish your more detailed budget as you will understand all the different costs necessary and will have chosen the main direction you want to take in your business so you will know what specific expenses you will have, as not all the expenses will be relevant to you that might be relevant to someone else. What I'm trying to say is don't try to be too perfect right now.

Exercise: Set Up Your Budget Template

I suggest that you set up a spreadsheet with the full list of expenses along the left-hand side and then have a budget column for each month and an actual column for each month. Here is an example of what mine looks like, and the one that you can download from the Online Resources (www.R2RGuide.com):

Category	Payee	Example Budget	Example Actual	January Budget	January Actual
Advertising	Business Cards	£10.00	£ -		
Advertising	Direct Mailing				
Advertising	Leaflet Delivery				
Advertising	Networking Meetings	£20.00	£40.00		
Advertising	Newspaper Ad				
Advertising	Online Advertising		£10.00		
Advertising	Other				
Advertising	Phone Answering Service	£10.00	£11.00		
Advertising	Postcards / Leaflets				
Advertising	Spare Room Membership / Ads	£10.00	£10.50		
Advertising	Website - Domain Registration				
Advertising	Website - Setup				
	Total Advertising	**£50.00**	**£71.50**	**£ -**	**£ -**
General Business	Bank Charges	£7.00	£6.95		
General Business	Business Insurance	£25.00	£27.00		

Once you've got the spreadsheet set up, let's talk about how to use it. I highly recommend that you have a budget and actual column for each month. You will use the budget column for recording how much you plan to spend for each item, each month. Ideally, you would set this at the beginning of the year and it wouldn't change unless there was a major change in the way you are doing business.

When you are just starting there will be some areas where you may overspend or underspend – that is to be expected while you are working out how to get the business started and learning the basics. When you are setting your budget I recommend that you be conservative. Therefore, if you know that business cards are going to cost between £50 and £165 every three months, then you put the higher figure into your budget. It's always better to underspend than overspend, and it's easier to reduce your budget in the future rather than increase it.

I recommend that as you go through the book you fill out each line on the spreadsheet so you can get an idea of the overall costs and then compare it to how much money you have to get started (see previous exercise). Then you can start cutting down and cutting out items so that the actual money you have to invest in the business is equal to or more than the amount you need to spend to get started. This is an excellent way to get a firm understanding of your start-up costs and whether you need additional funding (like joint venture partners) or you have enough to do it alone.

Then the Actual Column for each month is where you put what you've actually spent on each item during the month. This is how you make sure you are on track with your budget. It's important to do this at least monthly because it is so easy to overspend. You may think that you can add just this one extra piece of marketing or buy just one more training course, and if you aren't tracking it you will soon find that you have completely overspent and what you overspend in one area has to come from another area. This is fine, as long as you are making an educated decision about that and not just spending willy-nilly so that when you get to the end of the getting started phase and are ready to fund your first deal you then realise you don't have any money left. I've seen it happen before!

We've just covered the high-level basics of budgeting. I urge you to download the budget template from the Online Resources (www.R2RGuide.com) or create your own and update it as you go through this book. It is one of the most important internal business tools to help you keep on track!

1.4 Determine Your Rental Model

Rent to Rent is a sourcing strategy that you can use with a number of different property investment models. Some of the main ones are:

- Rent to Rent with HMOs (houses of multiple occupation)

    - With options of tenants: students, professionals, workers, benefits

- Rent to Rent with serviced accommodation

- Rent to Rent with LHA

- Rent to Rent with single family homes

- Rent to Rent with commercial units

And likely many more. The sky is really the limit here as Rent to Rent is just an underlying way to take control of a property and then use whichever property rental strategy works best to monetise the asset.

We won't be going into detail about the different rental models – that is the research you will need to go away and study to determine which best suits your goals, location, lifestyle, etc. I want to use this section to point out the importance of planning in advance what underlying rental model you will be using so that you can properly complete your business plan and focus your marketing efforts in the beginning.

Focus is one of the most important qualities you need to have when getting your business started. There are so many amazing strategies and opportunities out there – I know, I see them constantly – and the more you are out networking and building your business, the more opportunities you will be presented with. Most of the top business people and entrepreneurs will tell you that focus is a key trait to cultivate for any business. You need to pick one strategy/ business model and make it work before moving on to another one. I'm not saying that you can never move on but you need to make sure you take one strategy all the way through to completion and success before moving on to another one. Therefore, if you choose the Rent to Rent with HMOs model you need to focus only on HMOs until you have reached your target and the properties are up and running with your team and systems in place so that you can remove yourself from that business (i.e. you are working on the business and not in it) and then you can move your focus to the next strategy.

I see so many people trying to do both HMOs and serviced accommodation and yes, it can work, but you'll be tired and stressed as they are two very different underlying rental models with different systems and tenant needs. It is much smarter from a business standpoint to just do one at a time. Also, when you split your focus like that it doesn't make your marketing any easier as you have to explain two different business models in all your marketing material, websites, and presentations. It's much better to just get really good at one of them, master it and then move on.

Now, you might already be feeling hemmed in by the thought of choosing one strategy. I know how you feel – I get bored very easily and love moving from project to project (sometimes before I should…) so I know how frustrating it can be to be told to only focus on one rental model. But I strongly believe this to be a key factor to success and we have followed this in our business. Our Rent to Rent business focuses on the HMO model (young professionals) and this is the only strategy we focused on when sourcing properties and building our business. When we set up our business plan and looked into the future we knew we wouldn't want to do Rent to Rent forever – we knew it was just our getting started strategy. So we also wrote in our business plan that once we hit our Rent to Rent with HMOs target we would move on to purchasing HMOs, and then once we reached that target we would move on to flips/developments. That way I knew there was a plan for not doing only Rent to Rent forever and it gave me a framework to work towards. I suggest you do something similar and monitor your progress towards your initial end goal and have a measurement point of what needs to be in place before you can move to the next strategy.

Exercise: Determine Your Rental Model

Spend some time brainstorming on what the different types of rental models are and what you can do with a property after you've signed the Rent to Rent contract with the owner. What are your options? Make a big list of everything and don't get bogged down in the detail here and start thinking of the HOW – just focus on WHAT the different options could be.

Then once you've got a big list, I suggest you set it aside until after you have finished the book. Mark a date in your calendar to review this list (make sure you have finished everything else in the book) and then go back to the list and start researching how you can learn more about the rental models and start narrowing down to the ones that are best suited to your area and you want to get started on now vs. ones that might be great to look into in the future.

STEP 2:
SET UP YOUR BUSINESS

With a firm plan in place and goals set we can start to dig into the detail a bit more of what the exact steps are that you will need to take to put your plan into action.

Remember our quote from the last step:

> *A dream written down with a date becomes a goal.*
>
> *A goal broken down into steps becomes a plan.*
>
> *A plan backed by action makes your dreams come true.*
>
> Greg S. Reid

This is the action part of that quote and the rest of the book will have the getting started actions to take you down the path to making your dreams come true. You may already have started on some of these action points or some may not be applicable to you, although as a default I would say that from the legal section you will want to implement all of the steps. But even if you have started I still urge you to read through everything and make sure you keep your business plan updated with anything you need to do.

Also, I suggest you set up a basic Action Plan or task list where you can note down all the things that you need to do. There is a downloadable Action Plan in the Online Resources (www.R2RGuide.com) or you can create your own as a place to have a master list of all the actions you need to take to get your Rent to Rent business set up.

2.1 Understand the Legal Requirements

There is always a legal framework and some admin work to do around setting up any new business. One of the biggest hurdles for a lot of people with this is overwhelm, especially around a topic like legal requirements where it is very important for people to get it right. I urge you to keep it as simple as possible in the beginning and I'll give you tips on the easiest way to go. I'll also provide some options for people who love to have options so you can feel like you are in control and making your own decisions. No matter what your preference, these steps should not be deliberated over at length or take a significant amount of time. Many of them are just filling out some paperwork so any delays are likely to be of your own making.

If you find that you are struggling to get through this section and take action it might be worth spending a bit of time on your mindset and see if there is anything internally holding you back. This is one of the easiest sections of the book as you really do just need to follow the step by step instructions and there isn't a lot of wiggle room or creativity needed here. Just take a breath and take action.

Check the Online Resources (www.R2RGuide.com) for some of my favourite books about mindset and moving forward if you do find yourself wavering in this section.

2.1.1 Registering for Data Protection with the ICO

Registering with the Information Commissioners Office (ICO) for Data Protection purposes is a must do for any business in the UK that is collecting or storing data on individuals. This is as a result of the Data Protection Act (the Act). This data is anything from phone numbers to date of birth and any other personal information about people.

A few definitions from the Act:

DATA MEANS INFORMATION WHICH: –

    a) IS BEING PROCESSED BY MEANS OF EQUIPMENT OPERATING AUTOMATICALLY IN RESPONSE TO INSTRUCTIONS GIVEN FOR THAT PURPOSE;

    b) IS RECORDED WITH THE INTENTION THAT IT SHOULD BE PROCESSED BY MEANS OF SUCH EQUIPMENT;

    c) IS RECORDED AS PART OF A RELEVANT FILING SYSTEM

OR WITH THE INTENTION THAT IT SHOULD FORM PART OF A RELEVANT FILING SYSTEM;

d) DOES NOT FALL WITHIN PARAGRAPH (A), (B) OR (C) BUT FORMS PART OF AN ACCESSIBLE RECORD AS DEFINED BY SECTION 68, OR

e) IS RECORDED INFORMATION HELD BY A PUBLIC AUTHORITY AND DOES NOT FALL WITHIN ANY OF PARAGRAPHS (A) TO (D).

PERSONAL DATA MEANS DATA WHICH RELATE TO A LIVING INDIVIDUAL WHO CAN BE IDENTIFIED: –

a) FROM THOSE DATA, OR

b) FROM THOSE DATA AND OTHER INFORMATION WHICH IS IN THE POSSESSION OF, OR IS LIKELY TO COME INTO THE POSSESSION OF, THE DATA CONTROLLER,

AND INCLUDES ANY EXPRESSION OF OPINION ABOUT THE INDIVIDUAL AND ANY INDICATION OF THE INTENTIONS OF THE DATA CONTROLLER OR ANY OTHER PERSON IN RESPECT OF THE INDIVIDUAL.

Those definitions make it super clear, right?

You, as a Rent to Renter in your business, will most likely be collecting and storing personal data about people. This will include tenants and landlords. With tenants you will begin collecting their data even before you have properties as I'll show you in upcoming steps about marketing. You will want to be collecting their email and phone numbers so that you can contact them again in the future when you do have rooms available, and once you have properties and have them as tenants you will be collecting their date of birth, ID details, etc. So you definitely need to be registered with the ICO as this is considered personal data that you could use to identify them. If you have properties now and are managing your own tenants and are not already registered with the ICO, you must do this as soon as possible.

With landlords and potential landlords, you will be collecting and storing their data too. You will be setting up your marketing so that they are calling you and providing you with their contact details. Even if they tell you in the beginning that they are not interested in your services, you don't want to throw away their contact details. A no now doesn't always mean no forever so you do want to add them to your follow-up system.

Exercise: Register with the ICO

Registering is relatively easy and straightforward. It is something you need to do annually and there is a low annual fee (currently £35). You can find all the information on the ICO website – www.ICO.org.uk. You will need the following information to complete the registration:

    a.   Credit/Debit Card for payment (£35)

    b.   Company Name and Companies House Registration Number (if applicable)

    c.   Details about the type of data you process

    d.   Details about the number of staff you have

    e.   Details about your turnover (revenue)

Again, this is something you MUST do as part of your business. I suggest you do not put it off – take about 30 minutes to go through the set up process, add the annual fee into your budget and just get it done as soon as possible. I've included a step by step guide for registration in the Online Resources (www.R2RGuide.com).

2.1.2 Joining a Redress Scheme

New legislation was put in place on 1 October 2014 which states that every property manager and letting agent in England is legally required to join one of the three redress schemes approved by the government. Basically, if you are managing a property that you don't own then you need to be a member of a redress scheme. The mandatory requirement to join is to help raise standards across the lettings industry. It allows individuals (landlords and tenants) to lodge their complaints to an independent person with regard to the kind of service provided. The three schemes that property managers and letting agents can choose from are:

- The Ombudsman – Property Services

- The Property Ombudsman

- The Property Redress Scheme

If a complaint is made against someone and it is found to be true, the redress scheme can ask for an apology from the accused, issue a reprimand, order him or her to pay an amount in compensation, fine him or her, or the member can be expelled.

The following is some basic information on how to join the different schemes. You only have to join one of the schemes and they are essentially very similar so don't get too bogged down in the detail.

The Ombudsman – Property Services
(www.ombudsman-services.org/property.html)

This organisation deals with all property services (including chartered surveyors, surveyors, estate agents, residential managing or letting agents and valuers) and is a private, not-for-profit company that is independent from the property industry. They are members of The Ombudsman Association (formerly the British and Irish Ombudsman's Association (BIOA) which recognises them as independent.

Companies that want to register with Ombudsman Services can do it online. You will be required to submit an application along with a deed poll. The deed poll is simply a kind of contract signed between your company and Ombudsman Services stating that you agree to comply with their terms of reference. When applying for membership, you'll be required to present information about your turnover because this will help them to calculate the subscription fee you need to pay.

When you sign the deed poll and send it together with the pro forma invoice, you will receive an email to the effect that your membership application has been successful.

The amount charged for the annual subscription depends on the type of business you operate and in which month of the financial year you join the scheme. The financial year for Ombudsman Services runs from 1 April to 31 March. If you join after April they reduce the fees proportionately. My membership is around £200 per year.

Note: This is the one that I use.

The Property Ombudsman
(www.tpos.co.uk)

When you join The Property Ombudsman, you are required to choose the particular membership that is suitable for you and your business. There are different types of membership under The Property Ombudsman which include residential sales, international sales, commercial sales and lettings, residential property buying companies, residential buying agents, chattels and lettings.

The membership fee you are required to pay is currently £294 which is inclusive of VAT. There are some requirements for applying for membership and they include:

- Professional indemnity (PI) insurance

  You need to present a copy of the PI insurance schedule you are using and this should be about one to two pages. You should make sure that your indemnity is £100,000 or more although it shouldn't have an excess of above £1,000.

- Proof of identification

  A VAT number or company registration number is sufficient. If you don't have them you'll need to produce a copy of the latest invoice addressed to the company or the latest utility bill. In addition to that, you will need to present a copy of your passport or driving licence.

After producing these documents, you can apply for membership. You'll have to download the application form which you will then print and complete. If you are applying online, then you will have to scan the required documents before attaching them.

The Property Redress Scheme (PRS)
(www.theprs.co.uk)

The Property Redress Scheme is the newest redress scheme available. They are authorised by the Department for Communities and Local Government to offer redress to lettings and property management agents and the National Trading Standards Estate Agency Team (formally the OFT) to offer redress to estate agents. This is probably the simplest scheme in that there are no barriers to entry (i.e. required trade memberships or insurance requirements) and it is more affordable to join than the other schemes.

This scheme comes with two choices for agents which are Entry and Enhanced. The enhanced model (£199+VAT per annum) has no complaint fees while the entry model (£95+VAT per annum) does have a fee for assessing each complaint. It's up to you which you choose and you can easily join online.

Exercise: Join a Redress Scheme

Register with your chosen redress scheme. I suggest you do not spend a lot of time on this as it is something that you MUST do and there is not a vast amount of difference between the schemes. If you don't know which one to choose or don't want to spend time on it then I recommend The Property Redress Scheme. It is the newest scheme and from what I have heard it is the easiest and cheapest to join (I'm not a member of this one as it wasn't available when I started my business, but if I were starting over again today this is the one I would choose).

Again, don't spend a lot of time mulling over your choices as these are all very similar. Just pick one and go with it and if in doubt choose the PRS scheme.

2.1.3 Getting the Appropriate Business Insurance

There are a few different types of insurance that are applicable to business owners. Each business will be structured slightly differently and so you will need to spend a bit of time getting to grips with your insurance requirements. In this section I can give you a few of the highlights of the main types of insurance that might be relevant but I am not an insurance broker so I cannot give you advice in this area and none of the following should be considered advice. I suggest you speak with an insurance broker about your specific circumstances. An insurance broker is knowledgeable in this area so he or she will be in the best position to advise you on a policy that will cater to your needs. I have a couple of broker recommendations in the Online Resources (www.R2RGuide.com).

Public Liability Insurance

If you have a business (which you do as that is what we are setting up) then you need public liability insurance regardless of its size or structure; both limited company and sole traders need insurance. Someone can make a claim against you or your business for a number of reasons such as damage against property or individuals, or if they are accidentally injured at your premises. This is where this insurance comes in to protect you and your business.

This type of insurance covers your business as a whole – not on a property by property basis. Your landlords (the property owners) are still required to have their own form of liability insurance, which is generally included in their landlord buildings insurance. Again, refer them to an insurance broker if they have any questions.

The cost of business liability insurance depends on the amount of potential risks outsiders face from your business. Some of the factors that insurance companies consider when determining the premiums for cover include the nature of your business, the size and location of your business. One essential factor that determines how much you pay for cover is the revenues generated by your business, which you may need to estimate for the first year.

Most business owners make the mistake of thinking they do not need public liability insurance because of the size of their businesses or because they don't think their business poses a threat to outsiders. However, it only takes something as minor as a fussy tenant tripping over some wires in your property and losing a nail for you to be sued for injury. Therefore, every business needs business liability insurance.

Professional Indemnity Insurance

Professional indemnity insurance covers the advice you give to people. This type of insurance is common amongst professionals such as solicitors and accountants. You will need to consider your business model and whether you believe you are providing advice (to tenants/landlords) and, more importantly, if others will consider that you have given them advice. I personally don't feel like I am giving advice when I'm speaking to any of my clients (tenants or landlords) but I do have professional indemnity insurance because I want to be covered in case they believe I have given them advice. This will kick in if they act on the 'advice' I have given them and suffer adverse results. Speak to your insurance broker about whether this type of insurance is right for your business.

Employers Liability Insurance

This is mandatory as soon as you have an employee (other than yourself). There are many different definitions of employee so you will definitely need to review your situation and discuss it with your insurance broker. Here are a few things you should think about:

- If you have a limited company with more than one director you need to have employer liability insurance.

- Some subcontractors can be considered employed by you. This could be a self-employed contractor that you take on to do some admin, or a tradesperson, and if they are considered an employee of yours will depend on a number of factors including who is supplying any materials.

Employer liability insurance covers the health and safety of your employees and any loss as a result of an employee being injured while doing their job.

The cost will depend on the risk in your business and again (sorry I keep harping on about it) your insurance broker will be able to help you get the right insurance at the best rate.

Exercise: Work with Your Insurance Broker to Find the Right Policy for Your Business

I've listed out the three key types of insurance that you should consider first for your business – there are many others. It is important to discuss your specific business and circumstances with an insurance broker to find the right insurance for your situation. Also, it is important to note that every insurance policy has conditions covering their policy. You need to take the time to read through these conditions to ensure that you understand the terms and that they are suitable. Please see the Online Resources (www.R2RGuide.com) for my recommended brokers and contact them at your earliest convenience as you want your insurance in place before you start working with tenants and landlords.

2.1.4 Getting Legal Contracts (for use with Landlords and Tenants)

Having the correct legal contracts and documents is important for every business. There are some fees associated with this, but due to its importance it should be included in every business's initial start-up budget. We won't go into all the details of what needs to go into your contracts as there are template contracts available through the Online Resources (www.R2RGuide.com) but we will cover the high-level details about the different types of contracts so you can decide what is right for your business.

Contracts with Landlords/Property Owners

This is a section taken directly from my first book, *Rent to Rent: Your Questions Answered*. If you have not read it, it is a Q&A style book covering the top questions I was asked about Rent to Rent – from start to finish. I highly recommend that you check that book out once you have finished this one.

. . . .

From Rent to Rent: Your Questions Answered:

Let me elaborate a bit more on the different types of contracts you can have between yourself and the property owner:

(1) AST (Assured Shorthold Tenancy) – not recommended for Rent to Rent unless it has been specifically tailored for you by a solicitor who has experience with Rent to Rent. An AST is the

type of agreement that you would have with your tenants, not with the owner.

(2) Commercial Lease – this is great when the property owner doesn't have a mortgage as many mortgages don't allow long-term leases. Again, this should be drafted by a knowledgeable solicitor and can be written to contain whatever clauses and terms you and the property owner agree on.

(3) Management Agreement – this is the type of agreement letting agents will have with their landlord clients. This is more suitable when the owner has a mortgage as it is more commonplace and mortgage companies are used to management agreements. I still recommend that you have a good solicitor draft your agreement. Please note that if you use this type of agreement the income that you receive is management income and not rental income. Therefore, it can attract VAT. Please make sure you talk to a good accountant.

(4) Company Let Agreement – this is another type of contract that is generally not suitable for Rent to Rent. A company let is when a company rents a house from the owner to be used by THEIR employees. Since you won't be putting your employees in the house you shouldn't use this type of agreement.

We use a mix of management agreements and commercial leases. We prefer commercial leases as the income generally doesn't attract VAT for us, but we tailor our agreements to the property owner's situation as much as possible.

Ultimately, it is up to the owner to make sure their mortgage and their insurance are suitable. In all my contracts I make it clear that it is the owner's responsibility to maintain the property's building and landlord insurance along with telling them to ensure their mortgage product is correct.

. . . .

Ultimately you will need to understand the property owner's situation and needs in order to determine the correct contract and clauses for that contract. You can be as flexible or as structured as you like. I prefer to provide them with my contract as a fixed document and only change it if the owner asks. Most of them rarely ask for changes as they would be used to dealing with letting agents who would just have one standard contract. I've found the more I tell them the contract can be flexible and try to change it to suit them, the more worried they are about its legality. People like a standard document that you can say is used by all your clients and has been drafted up by your legal team. Keep it simple!

Contracts with the tenants

Your tenant type will play a large role in what type of contract you use with your tenants. Because it can vary so much I'm going to focus on a couple of common points on contracts for non-commercial tenants. If you are doing Rent to Rent on a commercial premises, then you will need specialist advice as commercial agreements are much more flexible.

For residential tenants (this could range from single families, through to HMO tenants, through to holidaymakers) I believe there is one basic question you need to ask yourself: Is this a Housing Act tenancy or a non-Housing Act tenancy?

- Housing Act tenancies – these are tenancies that are regulated by the Housing Act 1988 and require the use of an Assured Shorthold Tenancy Agreement (AST)

- Non-Housing Act tenancies are tenancies that are not regulated by the Housing Act 1988

Most residential tenancies in England & Wales are regulated by the Housing Act 1988. There are a few exceptions of tenancies that would **not** require an AST, as follows:

- The tenant's rent is over £100,000 a year

- The tenant is a lodger living in your home

- The tenant is a limited company

- The property is not the tenant's main home (Monday to Friday contract worker)

- It is a holiday let (weekend cottage/short stay)

If your tenancy with your tenant falls into one of the categories above, then you will be able to use a licence-type agreement. Check the Online Resources (www. R2RGuide.com) for my recommendations of where you can get your agreement. For the more common types of non-Housing Act tenancies there are many options for getting an agreement quickly and easily.

If you are in any doubt as to which type of contract you should use, then I suggest you use an AST. Many people, especially with HMOs, try to use a licence agreement for all tenants because they believe it is easier to evict tenants. With a standard AST there is generally a minimum two-month notice period that you (as the landlord) can give to the tenants to have them leave – and if they don't leave there is a specific procedure you need to follow to regain possession of your property. With a licence you are able to give the licensee just two weeks' notice to vacate but if you have any issues down the road and you end up in court with your tenant and it turns out you have used a licence agreement when you should have used an AST, the judge will simply follow the Housing Act 1988 rules and treat your contract as an AST. If you've been on any of the online property/landlord forums you will likely have seen discussions around the AST vs. Licence debate and opinions can run strong. Ultimately it's up to you to determine the risks you are comfortable with in your business. I tend to use all ASTs, even for tenancies that could have a licence, because it's easier for me to work with just one standard contract and I always know my contract will be fair to my tenant and myself.

Exercise: Get Your Contracts Sorted Ahead of Time

A lot of people wait to get their contracts drawn up until they have a deal ready to go. I think this is because they are looking to save money in upfront costs. I'm going to suggest you work differently from most people. If you are truly committed to this business and are taking it seriously then you should get your contracts now. I found it to be a lot easier to answer questions from agents and landlords once I had a contract and knew what it said. A lot of their questions are answered by your contract (e.g. What happens if I go bankrupt/don't pay the rent?). By already having a contract and understanding the terms of it will give you additional confidence when talking to agents and landlords and will give you more credibility. So I highly recommend that you get your contracts now – ideally both a management agreement and a commercial lease agreement.

If you go to the Online Resources (www.R2RGuide.com) you will find the contact details for my recommended solicitor along with a link to our available template contracts.

2.1.5 Determine Your Business Structure (Sole Trader vs. Limited Company)

I'm regularly asked how people should set up their Rent to Rent business – whether they should operate as a sole trader (or partnership) or a limited company. Ultimately, the choice is up to you and will depend on your business and personal circumstances. The same structure is not right for everyone.

You can do Rent to Rent as either a limited company or sole trader (or partnership if you have a business partner/s). I'll give you a brief summary of some of the pros and cons and what my experience has been.

Limited Company

A limited company takes more time to set up and has more legal and accounting responsibilities. You will need to file annual reports and the cost of doing this is generally higher than the cost of the reporting and tax requirements as a sole trader. With the additional reporting and accounting requirements there is the possibility of achieving more beneficial tax structures when using a limited company.

Another benefit of a limited company is that it limits your personal liability if things were to go wrong. That being said, you should never go into a deal with the attitude that if it all goes wrong then you can just walk away. That's the type of attitude that has given Rent to Rent a bad name with rogue operators setting up companies without the proper knowledge and research and then just running off when things go wrong, leaving property owners and tenants to bear the brunt of the distress. Always go into a deal after having done the appropriate research and believing 100% that it will succeed.

I operate my Rent to Rent business through a limited company and have personally found that it increases my credibility with landlords and agents. Even though it limits my personal liability to the landlord, they find it comforting that I have a limited company as it makes me seem more of a real business.

Sole Trader

A sole trader (or partnership) is easier to set up so you get started quickly and move forward. It has less onerous reporting requirements compared to a limited company (although you will still need to do a tax return and keep track of all your incomings and outgoings).

A downside of being a sole trader (or general partnership) is that it does not limit your liability so if things were to go wrong you could become personally liable. While I never go into a deal thinking that it will fail, I prefer to limit my liability as much as possible. Some landlords and agents find it less credible to be a sole trader.

We run our Rent to Rent as a limited company. This is mainly because I had a limited company set up already for my accounting consulting business so I simply changed the name from J. Edwards Accounting Ltd. to JADE Property Solutions Ltd. and off I went. I also have a background in accounting so the additional bookkeeping and reporting requirements were not as onerous to me as they might be for others. Finally, for my personal tax situation and my partner's it is more beneficial for us to work through a limited company as we are able to manage our personal income and retain profits within the company. This is the biggest thing that will vary by person. When you are just starting out and don't have a high income, some of my clients have had their accountant recommend to start as a sole trader as that will be more tax beneficial for them. You can always change to a limited company at a later stage.

Exercise: Determine Your Business Structure

Review your business plan and understand your future goals of the amount of profit you want and how best to structure that. I highly recommend that you speak with a knowledgeable accountant at this stage, an accountant who understands property investing and Rent to Rent with whom you can talk through your current situation and your future plans so they can help you to structure your business properly now and in the future to help you accomplish your goals. If you check out the Online Resources (www.R2RGuide.com) there is a bit more information to help you decide along with the contact details of my accountant. I'll also share my go-to resource for easily (and cheaply) registering a limited company.

2.1.6 Open Your Dedicated Bank Account and Start Your Bookkeeping

We discussed your business structure in the last step. If you've chosen to structure your business as a limited company, then it is mandatory for you to open a specifically designated business bank account. These generally have a monthly fee associated with them (generally waived for the first 12-18 months). If you are a sole trader, you have more flexibility and I suggest you start with a normal personal bank account as these don't usually have monthly fees, but make sure that it is separate from all of your day to day personal expenses. You need to have a bank account that you use only for your Rent to Rent business; anything else will result in a bookkeeping nightmare in the long term.

With regards to bookkeeping there are a few different options. If you are just starting your business, then keep it simple and just use spreadsheets. I've already taken you through a simple spreadsheet for budgeting and comparing your budget to your actual expenses (1.3. Establish Your Budget) and that should be part of your regular bookkeeping. You will also want to track cash flow as one of your most important measures. If you aren't great with spreadsheets or don't know what you should be tracking, then check out the Online Resources (www.R2RGuide.com) for some example spreadsheets I've put together for you.

If you already have some properties it might be time to start looking into some accounting/bookkeeping software. There are some really great and easy to use cloud-based software solutions. They are so simple that you may be able to set it up yourself and easily reconcile with your bank account. The Online Resources (www.R2RGuide.com) has some examples of bookkeeping software and some of my recommendations.

The final stage if you already have a large and thriving business and are using bookkeeping software is to outsource and make sure you have someone else doing the day to day bookkeeping and that you are able to dip in and check the financial statements on at least a monthly basis along with some Key Performance Indicators. I'm going to assume you aren't at this level as this is a Getting Started book.

====

Exercise: Get a Bank Account and Start Your Bookkeeping

This section is really short and sweet because there isn't much more information you need to get started.

1st – research what type of bookkeeping you'd like to start with and then use in the long term. The reason I suggest you start with your bookkeeping system is that if you plan to move to an online cloud-based bookkeeping system at some point in the future, it is a good idea to check out which banks are compatible with it and choose one of those as your bank provider. Once you have all your rents coming in and expenses going out of a bank account it can be very difficult to switch. So best to start with the end in mind and determine what your future bookkeeping looks like and select your bank account based on that.

2nd – open a bank account. Do a bit of research on banks if you'd like. As I mentioned above, it's best to choose a bank that fits in with your overall vision for your business and your business systems (i.e. bookkeeping). Some banks link more easily than others with bookkeeping software and it is best to not have to change in the future as trying to get all your tenants (and probably worst of all your utility providers) to update their payments and direct debits could be one of the most difficult things you will ever do!

2.2 Create a Professional Image

Once you've got the basic legal matters set up and in place it's time to give your business the professional image and credibility it deserves. There are quite a few steps in this section and whether you implement them or not will depend on your budget and personal circumstances. These are not all imperative to your business – in other words you won't be breaking any laws if you don't do any of the following. But they are more than just 'nice to haves'. The following steps are key to setting up a professional business and ensuring that others take you seriously. If you can't implement all of these steps now, then put together a plan that lays out when you will be able to afford them.

2.2.1 Choosing a Local Phone Number

You may be wondering why you need a local phone number when most people use mobiles now but while it's OK to have a mobile number available for clients, it is having a local landline phone number that will help your Rent to Rent business to look the most professional. Having only a mobile number can tend to make your company look less trustworthy and more fly-by-night, whereas a local landline number, especially if that phone is answered by a call answering service (which we will talk about shortly) can add a feel of permanence and credibility. This is especially useful if you are looking to conduct business outside of your home area as you can get a local number for any area by using a virtual service.

Many people are getting virtual phone numbers today because it works for residential and business users. Businesses especially have taken a special interest in these numbers. This is due to the fact that it enables you to form a local presence in an area without necessarily opening your office there. There are so many ways in which you can use a virtual number and most allow you to have calls forwarded to your mobile or any other phone number of your choice. This is the best option to allow for flexibility and growth in the future.

There are companies (check Online Resources (www. R2RGuide.com) for my latest recommendations) that charge from £10 per annum for phone numbers. However, if you want a number that is easier to remember then you can upgrade to a wider selection with charges from £95 paid in the initial year and then £20 yearly for renewal.

There are various types of virtual numbers so you should choose the one that is most suitable for your business requirements:

- 01/02 are the most commonly used numbers because they are local numbers. They advertise your business in any location with a local UK area code.

- 0333 numbers are convenient if want to make it cheaper for your customers to call you without the benefit of the client knowing your location. However, some people are uncomfortable calling 0333 numbers.

- 0800 numbers are free for your potential clients to call so are great for countrywide advertising. Again, I suggest you stick with a local number when you are getting started and only move to an 0800 number once you have a few locations that you are working in.

Exercise: Get Your Local Phone Number

Do your research and check the Online Resources (www. R2RGuide.com) for my recommendations for online phone numbers. Get an understanding of all the costs involved and how easy it is to manage your number and set up forwarding for it. There are products for every price range so make sure you use the budget tool we set up in 1.3 – Establish Your Budget and only purchase the phone number when you know how it fits into your budget. It can be difficult to cancel or move numbers, so once you choose a supplier you will be tied to it.

2.2.2 Gaining an Online Presence

In today's digital age it is imperative that you have an online presence. Most people expect to see a web address on business cards (which we will talk about later) and to be able to look at a website for basic information. You don't need to be selling from your website but they are important for building trust and credibility. You also need to consider your personal brand in the online space and make sure it is congruent with what your business is.

Let's look at personal branding first. This is important no matter what you are doing, from running a hobby property business to full-time sourcing agent to Rent to Rent landlord to property developer. You will need to keep your personal branding up to date as your business grows and evolves. Your personal brand is the 'you' that you want the world to see – to help them understand what you stand for and what you believe in. It will help people to get to know, like and trust you and to build your reputation as an expert in your field(s).

You don't need a special website for building your personal brand; I suggest you simply use the free social media tools that are available to everyone. LinkedIn is a must-have social media profile for this more professional focus on who you are. LinkedIn has some amazing tools for creating and sharing articles and posts with the world that will definitely build your credibility.

You also need to consider your Facebook profile as Facebook is an amazing tool for business – when used properly. Be careful about linking your personal and professional Facebook lives too closely as Facebook has some rules around this. I suggest that if you are starting to build a presence around your property/business persona that you start building a Facebook Business Page as the main place to share and build up your personal brand.

Slideshare is another great tool that is often overlooked. It is owned by LinkedIn but run from a separate platform. It's a great social media tool for posting presentations, articles and other marketing materials. Materials posted to Slideshare feature highly in search results and because Slideshare is owned by LinkedIn you can also cross-reference files between your Slideshare and LinkedIn profiles. Slideshare is a great place to put investor packs, example deals, marketing files, business plans and other documents that share who you are and how you can help.

For many people, when you are just getting started, building your social media presence will be enough. For others, a personal website will be the next step and you can use some of the same tips we talk about next.

Now we will cover your company brand and web presence. Most people and businesses don't need a fancy website with all the bells and whistles, especially when you are just getting started. The main purpose of most websites, especially for property investors, is to increase your credibility. You want to explain a bit more about yourself and your business to the world. Many people spend hundreds or thousands of pounds on their first website, then they wait weeks to months for it to be built only to be disappointed in the end with the results. Right now you just need to get a website up and running that gives a basic overview of your business and how it can help.

The quickest solution for your Rent to Rent business is checking out JADE Connect (www.JADEConnect.co.uk) where you can purchase a Rent to Rent template website based on the website I use in my business. This can have you up and running within a week with an easy and professional looking online image.

There are also some amazing tools that you can use to build your own website. These will take a bit of technical know-how and an eye for style but I do believe this is within the capabilities of most people using some of the tools I'll outline here. You can see more information on each of these in the Online Resources (www.R2RGuide.com).

1. WordPress (www.wordpress.org) is the norm for most people getting started with websites.

2. Weebly (www.weebly.com) is my top pick for those that want quick, simple and professional. With Weebly you simply pick a template from their beautiful designs and then you can easily add your own text and images without having to know any coding by using their easy drag and drop editing system.

3. Wix (www.wix.com/) and Squarespace (www.squarespace.com) are very similar to Weebly. They all have easy to use editors that don't require you to know any coding in order to build beautiful websites.

Of course there are downsides to building your own website. They take time and effort to build and to maintain. You won't benefit from the knowledge of a professional web designer who has studied and knows the ins and outs of websites. But I believe that generally the pros outweigh the cons in the lower cost, quicker start-up, and ease of edits. One of the biggest disadvantages I've had when having someone else build my website is that I was never able to just log in and make any changes. All changes required going back to the web designer and paying and then waiting for the updates to be made.

Exercise: Create Your Online Presence

It's time now to spend a bit of effort getting your online presence sorted out. For your personal brand this should have no cost outside of your time. If you are struggling to use social media there are some great courses you can take – check out the Online Resources (www.R2RGuide.com) for my recommendations. Make sure that your personal image and brand are consistent on all of the different platforms and that your message is clear on who you are and how you can help others.

For your business website there will be some cost involved. This is the time to research the options briefly and keep it as simple as possible. Make sure you check out the easy Rent to Rent template websites at JADE Connect (www. JADEConnect.co.uk) as I truly believe these are the easiest option. You aren't worried about SEO or online marketing at this stage; you just need a couple of pages for people to look at to prove you are a real company. If you are a bit more tech savvy, consider building your own website. Measure up the cost of all the options and make sure you add these costs (along with the ongoing cost of domain purchase, domain hosting, website updates) into your budget.

2.2.3 Setting Up a Professional Email

Are you trying to run your business by using a Gmail, Hotmail or other free email provider? Is your email address YourCompanyName@Gmail.com? If so, this section is very important because you need an immediate change. Having a professional email address is a huge part of taking yourself seriously because if you are still using a free email provider no one else will take you seriously.

There are many different ways of setting up a professional email address. This email is normally based on your domain name, which you will have set up in the last step (so your email could be YourName@YourCompanyName.com). Most domain providers and domain hosts will also host your email. They can be an easy option to set up straight away, but it is important to make sure the underlying host is reliable as you are relying on them to ensure the delivery of all your important business emails. You also want to make sure it is simple to use your email. Some providers require you to log in through their online web portal and it can be tricky to set up and re-route it through other servers so you can check your email anywhere (mobiles, tablets, etc.).

I have another option: G Suite. I love Google, I use them for everything! I had been using them for my personal email, calendar, and online storage for years before I started my own business.

When I started my first business (J. Edwards Accounting Ltd. which was my accounting consultancy business) I wanted to start looking more professional and I knew I needed a professional email address, not just my personal Gmail address. After doing a bit of research and spending a long time trialling other software, I found Google Apps for Business (the previous name for G Suite). Everything looks exactly the same as your personal Gmail Account, except you are able to have your own business domain. So now I have a professional email address but I can still use the same Gmail software that I'm familiar with and that syncs across all of my devices easily. In fact, I can still log in just by going to gmail.com.

I see so many businesses out there that are not taking advantage of this easy business basic. So many tradespeople have a generic Hotmail or Gmail address plastered on their van, like JoesBuildingCompany@Hotmail.com. That instantly makes me think it is a one-man band doing odd jobs around the house. And many of them aren't, they are just businesses that don't know how easy (and inexpensive) it can be to set up a professional image.

Exercise – Set Up Your Professional Email

I suggest that you check out the Online Resources (www. R2RGuide.com) for my step by step guide to setting up your professional email account with G Suite. There is also a link that will help you with a discount to the services to help make the start-up costs easier!

If you don't want to spend more money you can also check and see if email hosting is included with your domain name purchase or domain hosting.

2.2.4 Your Business Cards

Your business cards are one of the first bits of marketing material you can give to people. I recommend you make the most of them. You may need more than one depending on what you are looking for: property deals, investors, etc. First, you need a business card for your Rent to Rent business. This is the most important and is the card you can give to letting agents and landlords. It should look professional and be specific to your Rent to Rent business and how you can help landlords and agents. The following should be on your business card:

- Business Name

  - If you haven't got one, keep it simple. Make it easy to remember – don't try to make up new and clever words. Your name followed by Property Solutions is a common option.

- Business Logo

  - If you are struggling with this, again keep it really simple. It's quite common now to just use stylised font and have your business name as the logo. Otherwise, check out the Online Resources (www.R2RGuide.com) and I'll share with you my recommended logo programmes and designers.

- Your first and last names

- Your local phone number

- Your mobile number

    - You don't need to put this if you prefer people to call your local number first. I tend to leave my mobile number off my business cards because I'm not great at answering the phone and need time to prepare.

- Your email address

- Website address

- A photo of you

    - A lot of people want to skip putting their photo on their card. Do not skip this step. It's important to have a nice quality headshot of yourself that you can use on marketing material as it will help people remember who you are. It can be difficult to stay front of mind and, as they say, a picture is worth a thousand words. It's best to have a professional headshot taken, but if you aren't ready for that then use a nice selfie and have it photoshopped so that the lighting is bright and clear. This is what I did for my main marketing image.

Remember to make use of the front and back of the card. It's good to leave some white space (don't fill up every inch) but I suggest you find a couple of taglines that you can use to remind people of what you do and how you can help.

Once you've got your business card for your Rent to Rent business it's time to decide if you need any others. The next one I think you should consider is one for networking meetings. When you go to normal property networking meetings (like PIN or PPN) you are unlikely to meet landlords or agents that you will get Rent to Rent properties from. It's possible so make sure you bring your Rent to Rent business card, but it's more likely that you will be meeting other property investors. In this situation I think it is good to have a networking business card that shows how you can help or what you are looking for from other investors. For instance, are you looking for funds? You can gear your business card towards helping people find great deals or get great returns. Are you looking for deals? You can gear your business card towards that. Really consider what you want to get from going to the networking meetings and create a card that will help remind people of that when they go back through their stack of business cards after the meeting.

For your networking business card it is even more important to have your image on the card. Think about the last networking meeting you went to and how many business cards you left with in your pocket. If you even tried to go through them afterwards and remember every one, then most people you probably found it very difficult to remember everyone you spoke with. But if there is a picture of the person on the card it is much easier to remember a face than just a name. And if the card states exactly how they can help you it's even more memorable. So make it personalised and memorable.

If you have many facets to your property business you will want to consider how closely you want to run them. I've found that the more different things you tell people you do, the less they will understand and remember. Keep it simple – for both your future clients and partners and for yourself. Focus on one or two key things and be the master of those and be memorable.

Exercise: Get Your Business Cards

It's time to design your business cards. Consider carefully the messaging that you want on your business cards and what different cards you want to have. Your message will be different for each different type of target audience. Also, make sure you consider your budget!

The Online Resources (www.R2RGuide.com) section has some examples of my previous business cards for you to look at along with some tools to make creating your business cards really easy. I've designed all my cards myself using online tools, so if your budget is tight this is definitely the way to go. You'll see from the Online Resources that my first business cards were far from fancy (and they didn't have my photo!) but they did the job and as I tweaked them over time they got better and better results.

Make sure you consider your budget when deciding what types and how many business cards you need and consider how quickly you will get through them. It is often cheaper to buy most cards but if this is your first time ordering cards it can be better to order a small amount to start with to make sure you like the look and feel of them and also that your intended audience likes them. If you are like me, you may go through a few iterations before finding the design that you like best – so be flexible and don't buy 1,000 to start with!

2.2.5 Arranging a Call Answering Service

This is one of the 'nice to haves' in getting your Rent to Rent business set up. It adds significantly to the professional image and credibility of your company but it also adds a layer of additional cost that may not be right for your business. I recommend that you spend some time seeing how you can fit this into your budget as soon as possible as I have found the service invaluable over the years.

First of all, what does the answering service do? Well, it does what it says on the tin – it answers your phone calls. I have my local phone number set to forward directly to the call answering service. When it rings in their office it is then directed to one of their answering staff who also gets a message on their computer screen saying which business the call is related to and what your personal greeting and response options are. We also have a script that our call answering service takes landlords through to ask them for more information about their property. Once the answering service has taken a message they will immediately email/text you with the information. This service is invaluable for a number of reasons:

1. You don't have to worry about answering the phone when you are out and about. It would seem very strange if someone called your landline number and you answered from your mobile in Tesco with all the background noise. Definitely not the professional image you want to portray.

2. Your company sounds bigger than just a one-man band – adding to your credibility.

3. You have time to sit down and do a bit of research on the property before speaking with the owner. In the beginning (and even still a bit now) I am nervous speaking on the phone and having the first conversation with an owner/agent who is responding to one of my ads. It really helps me to have some time to look up the property and get a bit of an idea of what I'll be talking about before I speak directly to the potential client.

Again, this service can have an impact on your budget so it isn't something you need to set up right away. But as you step up your marketing (which we will talk about in Step 4) it is important to consider how you will handle all the incoming enquiries professionally.

Exercise: Consider Whether Call Answering is Right for You

Take some time now to do some research on call answering services. I've added a couple of my recommendations in the Online Resources (www.R2RGuide.com) including the company that we use. There may be different levels of service so review the options and put a few into your budget so that you can test them out and see how this service fits with the rest of your startup and ongoing costs. Once you have decided that this is the right step for you then get yourself registered and feel the pressure of constantly answering the phone be lifted from your shoulders.

STEP 3:
RESEARCH YOUR AREA

By this point you've got your plan in place and the basics of your business set up. You should know where you are at in your budget right now and have some flexibility built in for additional cost items in the next few sections. This section won't have anything that will impact your business set-up budget but we will be focusing on your area, which can have a high impact on your start up costs for your first Rent to Rent deal. But don't let the price of property in your local area affect too highly your selection of a Gold Mine area. As we will discuss throughout this section, I believe that working closer to home can be a much better option initially than working somewhere cheaper or that others say is better. I'll give you everything you need to know to assess an area to determine if it is right for you or not.

I also recommend that you only focus on one area at a time when you get started. It can be tempting to want to try out a couple of different areas just in case one doesn't work. But normally I've seen that result in none of the areas working. I tried it when I first got started and ran around trying to invest anywhere within two hours of where I lived. I spent so much time driving and setting up marketing and running Rightmove queries that I never had enough time to just focus on what I was doing and making it happen. Once I settled down and focused on one area (Oxford turned out to be my target area) I was able to focus my concentration, marketing and website on that target area, which made things clearer for my target audience (landlords and agents) and clearer for myself. And that's when the results started to happen.

A lot of the steps in this section are also covered in my other book, *Rent to Rent: Your Questions Answered*. I'll try not to repeat everything as you can easily find it all in there. I'll also make use of the free Online Resources (www. R2RGuide.com) more for step by step examples and videos so you can look through exactly what I do when researching an area. So let's get started!

3.1 Test Tenant Demand

One of the very first things you want to do when testing an area is to test the tenant demand. You want to make sure there are enough tenants so that you don't have to worry about losing money through voids. There will generally be a few voids here and there but in general when you are doing Rent to Rent you want to make sure these are kept to an absolute minimum.

Again, your method for testing tenant demand will be different based on your underlying model (HMOs, serviced accommodation etc.) and your tenant type (students, professionals, LHA etc.) and I can't go through how to test for all of them.

For my Rent to Rents they are mainly run as HMOs for young professionals so I test tenant demand using SpareRoom. SpareRoom is one of the most popular room rental websites in the UK and holds a lot of data. If you check the Online Resources (www.R2RGuide.com) there is a step by step walk-through of how to test tenant demand using SpareRoom.

If you are using an LHA or serviced accommodation strategy it may be best for you to get strategy-specific training on how to test demand and reduce risk of voids for those particular markets.

Exercise: Test Tenant Demand

First, you need to understand how to test the tenant demand for your particular tenant type and rental model. As I said above, I'll provide guidance in the Online Resources (www.R2RGuide.com) for how I test demand for my HMOs using SpareRoom. If you plan to use another model, I suggest you seek out specific guidance for that model/tenant type.

Once you understand how best to test demand then it is important to start testing. Usually the easiest way to test demand is by running dummy ads on whatever the most popular website is for your tenant type. The rental market is often seasonal so you will want to test as many different times of year as possible. I know that means you would have to test for 12 months, so you don't have to test everything before getting started. Just understand what seasonality (if any) there is in your market and adjust your results accordingly.

3.2 Understand Local Prices

Once you've assessed the tenant demand and are confident that you could fill your property and limit your voids, the next step is to understand the local prices of the rental market. This step will require you to get a general overview of your local rental market and will be strongly linked to Step 4: Do a Lot of Viewings. But in this step – before doing the viewings – it is important to get an idea of what is out there for your particular rental model (i.e. HMOs, serviced accommodation, commercial, etc.).

There are two sides of the market here:

1. The price you will pay to rent a property from the owner.

2. The rent you will be able to charge a tenant.

Understanding the Rent to the Owner

For residential properties Rightmove (www.Rightmove. co.uk) is currently the best place to be doing this as it is the largest online property portal. I also love Zoopla www.Zoopla.com) because I've found it easier to drill into the detail on their platform and look at comparables for neighbourhoods. And there are many other portals you can use as well – find the most popular for your market.

What you are looking to do in this step is get a general idea of the range in price of properties that fit your model. Using Rightmove as an example, set up a search for your target area and narrow it by the type of property that is best suited for your model – say if we are looking to do serviced accommodation that might be focusing on one-bedroom flats. Now you'll want to sort the search results by price and start going through to get an understanding of which ones are the most expensive, what area are they in, what condition are they in, and see if you can determine why they attract such a high price point. Then you'll want to do the same for the lowest priced flats. I've found that the ones on the lowest end have the most scope for a Rent to Rent as you will be looking to pay the least amount of rent to the owner to maximise your profits but understanding the top end of the market can give you ideas on how to get the most from your properties once you start renting them out.

I've created a template you can download to record the results of your research, which will help you organise it in a logical way and make sure you are analysing all the details. You can download it from the Online Resources (www.R2RGuide.com).

Understanding the Rent from the Tenants

Now we need to look at the other side of the equation and understand the rent we will be getting from the tenants.

At this point we will again be conducting the majority of the research online using the popular web portals for your niche. Continuing with the serviced accommodation model from above you will want to start looking at what other one-bedroom flats are being marketed for on the short-term market. Good places to look at are AirBnb, Booking.com, TripAdvisor, etc. I suggest you look through a few of the portals along with any local ones (cities like London and Edinburgh have local providers which can give great insight). Again, you'll want to target your specific area and limit your search criteria to the same that you used above so that when we come to running the numbers (3.6) we will be comparing apples to apples. You'll want to understand the daily, weekly and monthly pricing. Be cautious of seasonality and last-minute deals so check price points at multiple times throughout the year. You can set your search to look for properties available next week, next month, next quarter, etc. Make sure you are noting down all the key information for the cheapest and most expensive properties like: location, size, furnishings, quality, standards, amenities, etc. Never rely on getting the top market value for your property when you rent it out; keep your estimates conservative and make sure you understand the middle of the market prices.

Again, the downloadable template in the Online Resources (www.R2RGuide.com) contains space to note the above information.

Exercise: Research Your Local Prices

Using the downloadable template from the Online Resources (www.R2RGuide.com) take the time to note down all of the information listed above for your target market. You will want to do each different type of property separately (one-bedroom flats, two-bedroom flats, five-bedroom houses, six-bedroom houses, etc.) as you want to be able to make proper comparisons during Step 3.6.

3.3 Get to Know the Competition

Any time you are starting a new business it is very important to understand your competition. In your Rent to Rent business this is anyone who is letting out a property targeting your ideal customer. So if your customer (tenant) was not going to rent their property from you, who would they rent it from? That could be letting agents, other landlords, hotels, etc. It is impossible to check out everyone but you should get an idea of what else is out there. We did a little bit of that in the last step when we were checking local prices. You were mainly thinking of that step from your perspective of properties you would rent and prices you would get from your tenants but you can use the same portals to see where your potential tenants will be going and start to scope out your competition.

The purpose here is to understand the standards and prices of your competition. You will want to make sure you are a step ahead of them in the quality you provide at your ideal price point.

For example, let's use HMOs because that's my specialty. If you are going to use the HMO strategy with your Rent to Rent, you will want to know what other rooms are like in your area because if the tenant doesn't rent from you they will rent another room locally. First port of call for me is always SpareRoom to see what else is being advertised. Check out the ads to see what kind of text and images they use, check out the prices and what's included at that price and then get out and look at some of these properties. You are going to want to act like a potential tenant (or the parent/uncle/aunt) of a potential tenant out scoping around for a place to live. Set up a viewing of a few of the properties to get an inside look at what the houses and rooms are really like. This will be invaluable when you are setting up your own HMO as it will help you understand what else is really out there. Under no circumstances should you to try to pitch a Rent to Rent deal to whoever is showing you the property. This exercise is just to have a look around as a potential tenant. People might be a bit upset if you pretend to be a tenant and then arrive and try to sell them something – so don't do it!

If serviced accommodation is your model it might be a bit harder to actually get into the properties without actually booking them (and that can get a bit pricey). But they tend to have better images and more information about the accommodation online and you can also read the reviews left by people who have actually stayed in the accommodation. This will give you a great insight of what people like and don't like in their accommodation so you can make sure you set everything up with the customer in mind.

Exercise: Secret Shopper

I like to get into secret shopper mode for this exercise. You are going undercover to get an inside look at the competition. First, understand your target customer and rental market and target your competition by understanding who your tenant would rent from if they don't rent from you. Then research your competition online and in person if possible.

3.4 Estimate Your Bills

No matter which underlying model you are using in your Rent to Rent business (see 1.4) – whether it's HMOs, serviced accommodation or something else – you will have bills to pay. I'll cover some of the most common residential bills in this section and how I estimate them. The Online Resources (www.R2RGuide.com) will have more detailed videos and walk-throughs to show you some of the exact programmes I use.

You will need to estimate all of the bills as part of your costs for the property so that you know how much you can offer to the landlord in order to make the profit you are looking for. I'll list out the main costs and how to estimate them and then we will pull it all together in 3.6 – Running the Numbers.

Some of the most common bills you will need to pay are as follows – these are mostly geared towards HMOs/ serviced accommodation but should be considered in all other models and addressed in your contracts with both the owners and the tenants as to who is responsible:

- Council Tax

  - If you are managing HMOs either you or the landlord will need to cover the council tax. In a shared house it is not the tenants that are responsible for the council tax so it is important that you know who is taking care of it and be specific in your contract about who (you or the owner) is liable for it. I tend to take control of this as it's normally quite easy to set up on a direct debit. It's also very easy to estimate the bills as there are websites that allow you to look up the exact council tax rate based on the address of the property. One of them is www.mycounciltax.org.uk/.

- Gas / Electricity

  - I'll admit these are the bane of my existence. Utility suppliers are a nightmare! Their systems are a nightmare. Their customer service is a nightmare. Everything about them makes me want to tear my hair out in frustration. But you have to deal with them. I've got a commercial utility agent that I use and recommend and I'll put their contact details in the Online Resources (www. R2RGuide.com). Otherwise, I suggest you pick one energy supplier and stick with them. Changing is a horrible, horrible process.

Now that I've had a bit of a rant, let's move on to how we estimate our costs. For my properties I use a website called Glide to do my estimates. This is NOT who I used for my energy supplies and have never used them so I can't recommend for or against them but they are handy for estimating costs as they will do it based on the number of tenants for an HMO. I've also found that Glide produces a reasonably conservative estimate of what your bills will be – and I always like to overestimate my costs and end up with more profit later, rather than underestimating the costs and have a lower profit. Check out the Online Resources (www.R2RGuide.com) for a step by step walk-through of how I use Glide. It is quite simple to look at their website glide.co.uk/ and choose the Tenant Option and then you'll be able to enter the post code and address of the property followed by how many people will be living in the property and it will provide you with an estimate of gas and electricity. I normally ignore the other costs.

For serviced accommodation or non-HMOs it can be a bit easier to estimate your utilities. Most utility suppliers will provide you with estimates if you go to their websites and put in the post code and answer a few questions about the property.

For these general estimates before we have a property in mind just make it as general as possible so that we can set up an estimated budget. Then once you have a property in mind we can run the numbers specific to that project. More on that in section 3.6.

Another option for the gas and electricity is to set up pre-payment meters. Your tenant type will dictate whether this is appropriate or not but it can be much easier to manage if you leave the tenant in charge of paying the utilities. It is generally a much more expensive option but is very common when housing LHA/benefits tenants. If your tenants are paying the gas and electricity you don't need to worry about putting it in your budget.

- Water

  - Similar to the above for gas and electricity, it can be quite simple to estimate this using Glide or using your local water supplier's website.

- TV

  - The type of television service you provide will again depend on your tenant type. In some of our properties we only provide FreeView, in others we have Virgin Media Packages (or Sky). A lot of our young professionals don't watch TV in the communal area; they are more interested in streaming it from their laptops, which makes internet (discussed below) the most important aspect of any rental property.

You can estimate your TV costs by heading to the supplier's website. You can normally get a better deal when you bundle the TV service in with phone and internet. I would never provide a landlord phone for my tenants as everyone has a mobile now but in order to get the best price the landline is sometimes bundled in. Just don't tell the tenants and make sure you check the bills each month to make sure there are no unusual charges.

- TV Licence

    - Every house with a TV needs to have a TV licence. And technically if you rent the house out as an HMO where each tenant has a locked door and an individual tenancy, each room should have its own TV licence. We tell the tenants we take care of the communal TV licence but they are responsible for their individual room. There is a set price for all TV licences and you can find it on the TV Licence website www.tvlicensing.co.uk/. Once you've got a number of properties it could be easier to have a business licence and pay all the fees upfront once a year rather than managing multiple monthly payments. This is what we switched to once we got above 10 properties as it makes our administration easier.

- Internet

  - I've found this to be one of the most important parts of my property management: having the fastest internet available, especially in HMOs where there is a higher number of people using the internet generally at the same time. I tend to use Virgin Media as they have the highest speeds in my area. If you check the Online Resources (www.R2RGuide.com) you can get the name of my agent at Virgin Media who is used to dealing with bulk orders (i.e. people with more than one residential account). I tend to stick with getting residential accounts as I've found that the business branch of Virgin Media isn't very streamlined and it was difficult to get a quote and install set-up with them (and the prices weren't any better).

    I also provide the highest internet speeds in my serviced accommodation as well; the fewer internet issues the guests have, the fewer complaints you will have.

    So assess what your options are in your area and I recommend budgeting for the highest speeds in all your properties.

- Cleaning

  - For serviced accommodation this is a must. I also provide a bi-weekly cleaner in all of my HMOs to keep the communal areas in good condition and to help alert me to any issues in the property. If you have understood your competition from the last step then you will understand what services they are providing and you must, at a minimum, match that. Depending on your area, cleaning rates will vary from between £10 per hour to £20 per hour. I suggest speaking with a number of cleaners and get some recommendations from other local businesses on who they use. It's also best to use a cleaning company vs. a sole trader as you don't want to worry about finding cover if your cleaner is ill or goes on holiday. I have a company and they take care of all the people management for me.

So using your knowledge from the last section on what your competition is offering and understanding your tenant type, set your budget for how much you will need to pay a cleaner each month.

- Gardening

  - Normally tenants never look after the gardens. As a result, we make sure that we always arrange to take care of them. Similar to finding a reliable cleaning company, it's important to find a reliable gardening provider – someone with a small team that manages everything so that you don't have to worry about one person being ill meaning that none of your gardens get done. It's best to keep the gardens as low maintenance as possible and when you do find a property and it has a more complex garden speak to the owner about responsibilities and maintenance for any of the complex items that they particularly care about (hedges, flower beds, etc.). Your gardening costs will be more in the summer months than in the winter months but I tend to overestimate and just put the same amount in my budget each month. This can help give me a bit of a profit boost during those dreary winter months.

- Insurance

  - Finally, you should consider insurance. This isn't your business insurance, which we covered in 2.1.3, but this is the specific insurance for the property. First of all, the buildings insurance should be covered by the owner's policy. Make sure you specifically tell them the use of the property (HMO, serviced accommodation, etc.) so that they have the right type of insurance in place. I normally don't cover the cost of my Rent to Rent landlords' buildings insurance.

    What you should be considering for this section is any emergency cover you want. I generally take out a policy like British Gas Landlord Insurance when I first get started. This covers the boiler, heating, gas, water and electricity in the property. For around £30 per month per property I have peace of mind that any major maintenance will be covered by the insurance. You can have your landlord pay for this as well. I highly recommend this cover if you are responsible for the maintenance in the property. Even if you aren't it is a great service to offer to your property owner at not a high cost.

Once we got up to 10 properties we moved to self-insuring. This means that instead of paying British Gas £300 per month (£30 x 10 properties) we started putting that money aside into a separate maintenance account in our bank. We weren't having £300 per month of BG covered maintenance so this way we still have the money set aside to cover any unexpected costs, but any money we don't spend stays in our bank account and not in British Gas's pocket!

Another type of insurance that Rent to Renters consider is contents insurance. This would only cover your contents and not the tenants'. I generally don't get this (except for new appliances) as I don't see it as a high-risk area in my business with my tenant demographic. Speak to your insurance broker about this type of insurance and what it might cost you based on the type of furnishings you will be providing and your tenant type.

So those are the main expenses and where you can go to start putting together estimates of your monthly expenditure related to the bills. There are quite a few and this list is not exhaustive. You may not be responsible for paying all of these and there may be others that you should consider. It's important to make your contracts with owners and tenants clear about who is covering what and for now, in your budgeting, to ensure your budgets lean to the conservative side – as I'll show you in 3.6.

Exercise: Estimate Your Bills

Using the information above, make a list of all the bills you may be responsible for in your Rent to Rents. Consider your tenant type, your rental model and your competition. Do the basic research now and make a note of the different costs and options that are available to you and be ready to pull them all together in section 3.6. Also review the Online Resources (www.R2RGuide.com) for my downloadable checklist.

3.5 Become Familiar with National and Local Requirements

The rules are changing all the time in the rental market so it is very important to make sure you understand the current requirements. As I write this book there have been multiple tax and business changes that have impacted landlords across the UK and more are in the pipeline so I won't get into specific details in this section as they would soon be outdated.

It is very important for you to have a way of keeping on top of the changes and your local requirements. Each local council has the authority to implement their own specific rules that can cover their entire council or can vary on a street by street basis, which just adds to the adventure. This means it is important to stay connected to your local council, other local property investors, national property groups, etc. so that you are always up to date on the latest news and regulations.

Some of the key things to look out for depending on your ultimate rental model are:

- HMO Licensing Requirements – both mandatory and additional

- Article 4 Regulations

- Time limits on short-term rentals

- Planning Requirements/Change of Use

Exercise: Join Local and National Property Groups

Find a way to stay connected. There are national groups like the RLA (Residential Landlords Association) and NLA (National Landlords Association) that keep an eye on changing regulations around the country and provide valuable guidance for staying current and legal. There are also many local property networking groups that bring in speakers from around the country and provide access to other local investors that will be up to date with your local area requirements. Check the Online Resources (www. R2RGuide.com) for some suggested places to look for local groups.

Understand the cost of the different groups and memberships and add them to your budget to see which ones are possible to join now and will add the most value to your business.

3.6 Running the Numbers

In this step we are going to put all the numbers together and help you to assess a deal quickly – at a high level. You will need to do more due diligence once the deal passes this analysis, but this will help you quickly sort the wheat from the chaff so you don't spend too much time on properties that aren't really deals. And beware of another trap I've seen a lot of people fall into: analysis paralysis. If the deal doesn't stack don't spend hours and hours trying to make it stack. Not every property is right for Rent to Rent, or any property deal for that matter. Your job is to go out and get as many properties into the funnel as possible so you have more chances of finding the real deals.

So with that said, how do we quickly assess if a property is a deal? Here are my 4 Simple Steps:

1. What is the revenue you will be getting from your tenants? This is the rent that you will be able to charge and the total incoming cash per month from your tenants. Keep this conservative, don't

use the absolute highest market rate possible. Use a realistic average of what you know you will be able to get in a push if you need to fill the room quickly. Then if you are able to charge more it's a bonus, rather than a loss, if you end up not being able to get the top rents. You should also factor in any known void periods. For instance, with serviced accommodation you may be charging £100 per night, but you know you won't have 100% occupancy, so adjust your figures for expected voids. For HMOs be reasonable with voids. I've seen people budget for 10% voids, which makes their expected revenues really low and impossible to find deals. If you are expecting more than 5% voids you should really be looking into your area and seeing if you are in the correct market/have a correct understanding of your market. I'd say we generally fluctuate around 1-3% voids depending on seasonality.

2. What is the cost of bills? This includes all the utilities, property-specific insurance, council tax, TV licence etc. that you will cover every month whether you've got tenants in the property or not. Use the information you put together in 3.4 to come up with the total monthly cost of all your outgoings. Also, this is a good place to add in an estimate for any repairs and maintenance you will be responsible for, depending on what you want to agree with the owners. Some Rent to Renters take on all maintenance and some take on just a limited amount each month (like the first £100). Decide

what you would prefer to do in your properties and estimate how much you will be likely to spend on general repairs and maintenance each month. If you are just getting started this can be a tough number to estimate as you won't have anything to base this number on. Again, keep it reasonable – you likely won't have 10% monthly maintenance costs so don't put that in as an estimate. It will also depend on the current standard of the property so make notes when you do your viewing.

3. What is the profit and return on investment (**ROI**) you need from the property to make it worth your time and effort? ROI is calculated as the total annual profit divided by the total upfront costs. The monthly profit and the **ROI** will be different for everyone as we all have our own criteria and value of time and money. Here are a few rules of thumb:

    a. If this is your first deal don't limit yourself by only looking for deals that make £1,000 or more per month. Yes, those deals are out there but it's a lot easier to start with the deals making £500 per month and work your way up so you can build credibility and experience.

    b. For HMOs the rule of thumb is £100 profit per bedroom per month, so for a five-bedroom house you would be looking for a minimum of £500 profit per month. Also, you need to consider what your average room rate is and consider what would happen if that room were void for the month. Would you be in a loss position? If possible, try to make your profit more than your average room rate so that if there are voids you aren't losing money. This might not be possible in expensive areas like London, so make sure you understand your market so you can limit voids.

c. For serviced accommodation make sure you understand the seasonality in your market and that you factor in a void period. You generally want to make sure you are profitable at 60% occupancy and understand how you can cover the cost of any additional voids during slow seasons.

d. You will also need to consider how much you will need to spend upfront to determine your minimum ROI. This spend includes any deposits, upfront rent and maintenance/ refurb to get the property into the condition that you want. Will you need to buy furniture? Locks? Decorations? Crockery? White goods? List everything that you will generally need to provide and any property-specific maintenance requirements to get a full picture of what you will need to spend upfront before you start making any money from the property.

Generally, with Rent to Rent you are looking for an ROI of 100% or more, which means that you get all your money back in the first year and then every year after that is profit, but again everyone has a different number so you need to know your minimum ROI.

4. The rent paid to the owner (lease fee). Sometimes the owner will tell you the minimum amount he can take for the property and still be happy, but I've found that more often than not they want you to make them an offer. So normally I use this as the last number in my equation and as long as I know all the others (above) then I can calculate the highest lease fee that I can pay to the owner.

Let's run through an example so we can see how it works. I'll show you how I back into number 4 so that I can make an offer to the owner – we'll use an HMO as an example (for other examples check the Online Resources (www. R2RGuide.com)).

Example: HMO 1:

We've done the research from Step 3.1 and know that we want to house young professionals in HMOs. We've looked at our local area and have decided that there is a great patch within a mile around the local hospital where tenant demand is high for the professionals working at the hospital and that is going to be our target demographic.

We've also spoken with the HR department at the hospital and by building a relationship know that they always have staff looking for housing nearby.

Then we looked into the local prices (Step 3.2) focusing on SpareRoom as that is the most popular room rental portal in our area. Using the methodology from the Online Resources (www.R2RGuide.com) we've discovered that the average room rate for a double room in our target postcode (all bills included) is £500 per month. We verified this by getting out and looking at a few of the available rooms (Step 3.3) and doing a bit of secret shopping. By looking at rooms in different price brackets and standards we see that for a really high-end room you could charge £600 per month and for the smallest and lowest quality they are getting around £425 per month. So we feel that we can provide a good quality and easily receive the average £500 per month (likely we can charge more, but we would definitely be able to quickly fill rooms at the £500 per month rate, which is our conservative estimate).

Further, most four-bedroom houses of this size and type on Rightmove (Step 3.2) are marketed at £1,300 per month). We've found this one direct to vendor and we can see that they were previously advertising themselves on Gumtree at £1,700 per month and the ad is three months old.

We've estimated our local bills using the guidance in Step 3.4. Based on council tax rates and focusing on properties with five bedrooms, we estimate that the monthly bills will be approximately £550 per month (including a small allowance for repairs and maintenance).

Our local area does not have additional licensing or Article 4 and the property we are looking at right now only has two floors, so it doesn't fall into the current rules of mandatory licensing. At the time of writing this book there are changes looming so please make sure you know the current rules right now! We do want to make sure we are future proofed so we have checked that the property meets the minimum room sizes and has the appropriate facilities for five bedrooms should it need to become licensed.

Now we have found a suitable property: it's currently a four-bedroom house with two reception rooms, one of which we can easily convert and use as a bedroom so we have five bedrooms with a large kitchen/dining area. There isn't a lot of work needed as the owners just refurbished it but haven't been able to rent it out as they were only looking at families. It doesn't come furnished and there are a few changes we want to make along with giving the owner a deposit as this is our first property, so we estimate approximately £6,500 of upfront costs. We know we need a minimum of 100% ROI as we want all our money back in the first year of our five-year contract.

We need to calculate the maximum amount we can pay to the owners for the monthly lease fee.

Step 1 – revenue from tenants (5 rooms @£500 per month)	£2,500
LESS: **Step 2** – monthly bills	£550

LESS: **Step 3** – our minimum monthly profit (see below)
 	
Calculating ROI
    ROI at £500 profit per month:
        Annual Profit = £6,000 (£500 * 12)
        Upfront Costs = £6,500
        ROI = 92.3% - this does not meet our 100% minimum ROI
    ROI at £550 profit per month:
        Annual Profit = £6,600 (£550 * 12)
        Upfront Costs = £6,500
        ROI = 101.5% - this does meet our 100% minimum ROI & meets our minimum rule of thumb of £100 profit per bedroom per month.
	£550

EQUALS: **Step 4** – maximum amount we can offer to the owner.	£1,400

So based on our assessment and running the numbers above we can offer the owner a maximum of £1,400 per month and we would still be happy as we are making £550 per month. As we read above, they are currently advertising on Gumtree for £1,700 per month but the owner doesn't know you saw this as they called you directly from your newspaper ad and have asked you to make an offer. Based on this exercise you now know your maximum offer range and can start negotiations.

There is no specific exercise for this section. I recommend that you practise going through this exercise on some properties that you see online (on Rightmove or other portals) so you can get used to making assessments quickly. Also, you can build a spreadsheet that will help you analyse deals easily – or use the spreadsheet we've provided in the Online Resources (www.R2RGuide.com).

STEP 4:
DO A LOT OF VIEWINGS

Now we come to where the real magic happens! Everything up until this point was to prepare us and get us ready for the viewings. In Step 1 we made a plan, in Step 2 we got the business set up, in Step 3 we did our market research and now we are ready to get out there and start looking at properties.

Don't worry, we will go through the basics of marketing and what to say to people so you will know what to do. This is the place where many people feel the most nervous, so if you are feeling a bit scared about getting out and looking at properties, it's OK – you aren't alone.

I was absolutely terrified when I first got started in property and the thing that terrified me the most was making a mistake and sounding stupid when I was talking to agents and landlords. What if they realised I didn't know what I was talking about and that I had never done this before? But even with those fears I still had to get out there and do the viewings and explain to the agents and owners how I could help them, and it took a while to get the hang of it. I didn't get a deal on my first try, or even the second, third or fourth. In fact, it took about four months before we got our first deal signed. The most important thing is not to give up and to learn each time you go out. Look at the first few viewings as practice and learn from them. Understand what kinds of questions people will ask and watch how they react to your answers. Reflect on the viewings in the evening and write down what was good and what you can do better next time. This is a very important part of the process!

In this section we are going to walk through your marketing and how you get the viewings set up and then what you need to look for at the viewings. I'll give you a few tips about negotiating as well but you'll learn the most through actually getting out there and doing it! So let's get started!

4.1 Set Up Your Marketing Machine

In order to get viewings, we need to get our marketing machine set up. There are two main ways of finding properties: 1) from landlords/property owners directly and 2) through letting and estate agents. I'll cover both of them in this section and give you some great tips on exactly where to look and how to get started with your marketing.

It takes some time to get your direct to landlord marketing set up and generating results as most people need to see your marketing more than once before they will feel comfortable calling you. That's why we will cover that first so that you can get it up and running and then while you are waiting for the responses you can go out and start working with the agents because it's a lot easier to get in touch with them.

4.1.1 Direct to Landlord

As mentioned above, the direct to landlord marketing can take a while to start bringing in leads. Often people need to see your message more than once before they call. Marketing gurus say that you need seven points of contact to build the 'know, like and trust' factor with a client. So the more different types of marketing you can get out there, the better, but you also need to balance this marketing with your budget. Your marketing will probably be one of the most expensive items for your business, so you need to choose wisely. And in order to help you choose wisely you need to be tracking and measuring the results from your different marketing campaigns so that you know which ones are working and which ones aren't. For instance, if you are spending £100 per month on a newspaper ad and £500 per month on leaflets and you got 10 calls from your newspaper ad and one call from your leaflet after three months you may want to shift around your spend a little bit and focus more on the newspaper ad. So it is really important that you track the results and understand which leads come from which marketing method.

Also, it is impossible to say which method will work best for you without trying a few. You can talk to other local advertisers in your area to get an idea of how the different methods work for them, but the best way to find out is to try them yourself. I'll give you a few examples of the top ways I've used to get my message directly in front of landlords.

- List of licensed HMOs from the council. This was my number one best marketing method for my specific strategy (Rent to Rent with HMOs). I got the list of properties that were licensed by the council and was able to send the owners letters directly. This put my marketing message in front of my target audience month after month. And that is the key – continuously sending letters! Many people give up after one or two letters but remember, they need to see your message around seven times before they feel comfortable so I recommend sending the letters every four to six weeks.

- Newspaper ad – local classified section. We had good results with our newspaper ad as well. Make sure you are smart about placement and text as this can be an expensive method of advertising. I recommend you put your ad in the classifieds section of your local free weekly newspaper. This is the paper many people often have at home and keep it around all week dipping in and out. So a nice bright ad in the classifieds will stand out every time they flick through to see what's on offer.

- Leaflets. If you have a specific target area you know you want to work in, this can be a great method. The only downside when targeting for Rent to Rent is that you are often targeting rental properties so your leaflet isn't getting to the owner, but to the tenant of the property. So it's always helpful to add an incentive to pass the message along (something like: 'Know someone that might be interested? We pay £100 for referrals that turn into clients').

- Local landlord/business networking meetings. This is a great place to get leads. I'm not talking about the property investors meetings (like PIN or PPN) because they are generally people that are looking to do something similar to you. But if you head to the local NLA meeting (National Landlords Association) or the local Chamber of Commerce meeting then you are likely to be much more successful finding landlords that aren't as knowledgeable about the latest strategies and may be looking for some help. But do not go to these meetings with a sales attitude; the key to networking is helping others and truly listening to their story and their issues. If you go with an attitude of giving you will be received by the other members with much more open minds. It is not all about pushing your business card and dominating the conversation; it's about building relationships. Often at business networking meetings it's not about selling your services to the people in the room but building the relationships with those people so that they want to sell your services to their friends and customers. Just imagine making friends with an amazing accountant who works with high net worth individuals and maybe he needs a recommendation of a great handyman and you just happen to know the right person who does a great job for him. The accountant realises that you know your stuff after a few conversations and a few other helpful tips about how to get the most from his rental property and now he wants you to come and present to a select group of his high net worth clients. Jackpot! And you didn't sell to him but by helping him and building the relationship you opened up his network of people.

- Online advertising. This can go both ways: you can advertise on different online channels (Facebook, Google, local pages, etc.) and you can also scan online ads that landlords may be placing to find tenants (Gumtree, SpareRoom, etc).

In the first you will need to do your research on how best to use the different online marketing mediums and make sure you have your target audience set properly to get the most out of the advertising available to you.

In the second this is a great way to call a landlord directly. Be a bit careful as these landlords are looking for tenants and often don't want to work with agents so you need to position yourself well. And as I mentioned in the secret shopper section (3.3), never pretend to be a normal residential tenant and then turn up at a viewing and reveal yourself as wanting to do a Rent to Rent and start talking about managing their property for them. They will generally not be happy as they will feel you deceived them. So make sure you explain at a high level what you are doing before meeting. Section 4.2 has some scripts you can use to do this.

Exercise: Research Your Marketing Options

In this exercise, you should research all the marketing methods above and any others that are possible for your area. Do a brainstorm and make a big list of all the different things you can do to find leads (including bandit boards, bright yellow t-shirts, flyers at local shops, etc.). No matter how crazy, write it down and then put a price next to it. Sit down and figure out how much it will cost you per month to do each of those marketing methods. Then line it up with your budget and how much you have available to spend on marketing each month. Try as many of the different marketing methods as possible (within your budget and allowing for at least six months of continuous advertising with each method). Then make sure you track and measure the results so you know what is working and what isn't working!

4.1.2 Working with Agents

Working with agents can seem a bit confusing to many people because new Rent to Renters feel like they are competing with the agent and that the agent will immediately see it that way and not do business. But it is completely the opposite if you are able to build the relationship and position your business correctly as you can provide a valuable service to the agents. Also, you aren't competing with the agent and you don't need to pay them a separate fee (although you can if you want to).

When working with you the agent can keep their contract with the owner – just like they would with a normal tenant. Instead of renting the property to Mr & Mrs Smith the agent simply rents it to you (using your contract of course) but their position remains the same and their contract with the owner stays in place. So if the agent has a management (or agency) agreement with the owner to manage their property for a 10% commission, when they rent to a normal tenant the tenant would have an AST (Assured Shorthold Tenancy agreement) signed either by the agent or the owner. Then the tenant (Mr & Mrs Smith) would pay the agent the monthly rent – say £1,000 every month. The agent would keep their 10% and pass the owner £900 per month (less any maintenance, etc.). The situation remains exactly the same financially with your Rent to Rent agreement. The agent still has their original agreement with the owner to manage the property for a 10% commission, then you simply take the place of Mr & Mrs Smith (but use your commercial lease or management agreement that must be signed by the property owner). Then every month you pay the agent £1,000 and the agent takes their £100 commission and passes the remaining £900 on to the owner. And even better for the agent, when working for you they don't have to take any tenant phone calls or do any management as you take over all of that!

Normal Tenancy

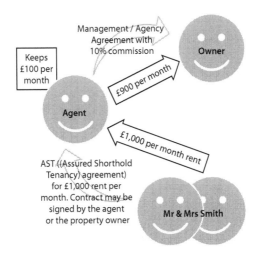

Management / Agency Agreement with 10% commission

Keeps £100 per month

£900 per month

Owner

Agent

£1,000 per month rent

AST (Assured Shorthold Tenancy) agreement) for £1,000 rent per month. Contract may be signed by the agent or the property owner

Mr & Mrs Smith

Rent to Rent

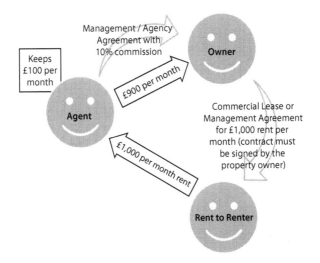

Management / Agency Agreement with 10% commission

Keeps £100 per month

£900 per month

Owner

Agent

Commercial Lease or Management Agreement for £1,000 rent per month (contract must be signed by the property owner)

£1,000 per month rent

Rent to Renter

So now that you can see how the agent can still benefit from a relationship with you, you can be more confident when approaching them and getting started. It can take a bit of time to build up a relationship with the agents. Some important tips:

- When visiting the agency in person, make sure you speak with the key decision maker at the agency. Sometimes you may need to make an appointment to come back and meet with them. Keep your explanations brief with anyone else as you don't want to muddy the waters. Simply leave them with a business card and your marketing materials and ask for a call back if they are unwilling to take you to the lettings manager right then.

- When arranging viewings over the phone or via email, understand that the person you do the viewing with is most likely not a decision maker and may not have a lot of information about the property. Again, don't go into a lot of detail with them, simply leave them with a business card and marketing material and ask for the contact details of their manager. When I'm at the viewing I usually say that because we work differently from just a normal tenant, it's best if we speak with their manager when making our offer.

- Understand that it takes time to build up a relationship and build credibility. Their business reputation is on the line and they may have been approached by less than scrupulous people in the past. Don't jump into bed on the first date with your agent as it is their professional duty to protect their client's interests. Be professional, explain how you can help, what your experience is and provide them with professional marketing material. Some people respond best to verbal explanations and some people need to sit down with written information in order to absorb it. Be able to provide both.

- Often it is easiest to work with the small independent agencies. Many of the bigger regional or nationwide agencies have their own legal team and strict processes and procedures that the team members (including managers) are unable to deviate from. They are also less open to new ideas. With smaller, independent agencies you are often able to deal directly with the owner/ director who is generally more open to ideas as long as they can see the benefit to themselves and to their clients.

- Practice makes perfect. The more often you are out viewing properties and talking to agents, the better you will get at it. In the next section I will provide some scripts to use to help you start the conversation.

Exercise: Get to Know the Local Agents

Make a list of the local letting agencies. Get a high-level understanding of their structure (are they local, regional, national, a franchise or independent, etc.?) Check where their offices are, what areas they cover, what types of properties they seem to specialise in, what their general terms are with owners (often agencies will publish this information on their websites). Also, review Rightmove and Zoopla and see which local agents offer the most types of properties that are suitable for your rental model. This exercise is to prepare you for the next step!

4.2 The Scripts to Get Started

Once you've set up your basic marketing and maybe you have some leads coming in from landlords or you've researched the agents and found a few properties on Rightmove, what happens next? What do you actually say to these people to get them on board? Or even just to set up a viewing? In this section I will give you a couple of scripts or outlines of what to say.

These scripts aren't for the end negotiation or to secure the deal. These are ideas for what to do before the viewing and to use a bit at the viewing to help explain at a high level what you do.

No matter what, when you are lining things up before seeing the property and even during the first viewing you want to keep things as simple as possible. Don't get into long discussions about how your business works and try to list every way you could possibly help them. Your goal is to listen more than you speak. Draw the other person out so that you can understand the agent's situation, the owner's situation and as much as possible about the property. A lot of us are really selfish and most people are only focused on themselves. We are all generally so worried about what people think about us that we miss the bigger picture in that our goal as a business is to help other people and in order to help other people we need to understand what the problems are. If we are too busy 'selling ourselves' then we walk away without an understanding of how we can help. So your goal is to listen more than you speak, and when you do speak you should be focused on understanding the other person. Let's go through a couple of scenarios.

First Call to Agent/Landlord:

This script works best when you've found a property on Rightmove that you are interested in and you are calling to set up a viewing, or if a landlord has replied to some of your marketing and you need to call him/her back to set up a viewing. In this situation you are calling the other party to learn a bit more about the property and to schedule a viewing:

> **You:** Hello – I am calling about your property at <123 Station Road>. I saw the property on Rightmove (or I received your message about the property, or explain how you know about the property).

> **You:** Can you tell me a bit more about the property?

> **Them:** They should tell you a bit more. Sometimes agents aren't very helpful, especially if it is just the office receptionist. Just have a short discussion to understand at a high level about the house. If you are speaking with the property owner, they will tend to give a bit more detail.

> **You:** Thank you – the property sounds great. Is it OK if I tell you a bit about me? (This is normal –

a landlord is going to be wondering who you are and agents often take notes about their clients to understand what other properties they might be interested in.)

You: I am a relocation agent based in <Your City>. I work with companies in the local area to help house their employees. We currently have more clients than we have houses so we are currently looking for properties like this. What we do is guarantee the rent for the landlord on a long-term basis and we become the tenant, similar to a corporate let. Is this something that you think the owner might be interested in?

Them: Ideally they will say yes they think that is something the owner would consider. Sometimes they will say no – try not to get into an argument with them or push too hard. Some property owners are only looking for short-term lets or some owners want to be more hands-on with their properties. While a yes is ideal, a no is OK too and you can move on either way by asking the following question.

You: Do you have any other properties similar to this that we could have a look at as well?

NOTE: You should understand the basics of your area by this point. You should know a couple of the businesses that your tenants will be working at so that you can answer any questions about who you work with. Or maybe you will be housing hospital employees, or students from the local university. Just know the names of the businesses/

hospitals/universities and be able to give a few examples. Again, don't get drawn into detailed conversations at this point. If the other person says: Oh – you work with XYZ Limited, my best friend is the HR director, you must work with them, it is OK to say that you don't know them. It is OK to say something like: My business partner/colleague focuses on that side of the business so I'm sorry I don't know that person. In fact, this is a great answer for any non-viewing-related question that they might ask. As part of a business you wouldn't normally be expected to know every single job role. Right now you might be a one-man band and you are doing everything but many companies aren't one-man bands and it is perfectly reasonable that there would be separate job roles for finding properties and filling properties.

Also please note that what you say needs to resonate with you. You need to feel comfortable and confident saying it. That generally takes practice so you won't do this perfectly the first time. But it also may take a bit of tweaking of the script. Not everyone feels comfortable or congruent saying that they are a relocation agent. So take some time to find what you are comfortable with as you need to believe in yourself and your business. Keep it as simple as possible and high level at this point. Here is another example:

> **You:** Hello – I am calling about your property at <123 Station Road>. I saw the property on Rightmove (or I received your message about the property, or explain how you know about the property).

You: Can you tell me a bit more about the property?

Them: They tell you a bit more...

You: Thank you – the property sounds great. Is it OK if I tell you a bit about me?

You: I am a property investor based in <Your City>. Because of my work with **XYZ** Company I have a surplus of tenants and not enough properties for all of them. So I am looking for a few more and what I do is guarantee the rent for other landlords on a long-term basis and manage their properties just like my own. Is this something that you think the owner might be interested in?

Them: Yes – that could work.

You: Do you have any other properties similar to this that we could have a look at as well?

If you find that the person on the other end of the line keeps asking detailed questions or seems to want a lot of information about exactly how everything will work, bring them back up to the higher level. It's OK to say something like: This is a lot easier to discuss in person once we have had a look at the property to make sure it is the right fit for us. I can bring one of our information packs to the viewing and we can talk through the details then. If they want to know more ahead of time you can also direct them to your website (that you set up based on Step 2.2.2) so they can see that you are a professional company with a professional online presence.

Exercise: Practice the Scripts

Practice makes perfect. First, tweak the scripts above so that they are comfortable and congruent for you and your business. Don't change them too much at first as these scripts do work. Just find the best words to explain your business; if you don't know then just use the scripts as they are.

Then find a buddy to practise with or start with an area that you don't want to work in and start calling agents and running through the scripts. Practise somewhere that it doesn't matter if you mess up. One of the most powerful exercises we do in my live training course is the time when everyone calls an agent about a property. When we come back to share learnings many people are amazed to realise that they didn't die, it was a lot easier than they thought, and people on the other end of the phone are generally nice people. Remember, the more you practise, the easier it will be!

Once you have tried it a couple of times with a buddy or out of area (don't spend more than a day on this) then you are ready to do it for real. Don't get stuck in practice mode. There are some additional scripts and tweaks that you can use in the Online Resources (www.R2RGuide.com).

4.3 Viewing Checklist

Now, what happens when you actually get to the viewing? There are a few key things that you need to know in order to make a strong offer and also a few seeds to sow in order to get the agent/landlord positioned to accept your offer. I don't recommend making a firm offer at the viewing because I always prefer to have some time to go back to my computer, check the numbers and come up with a full plan. I also see jumping into an offer right away as less businesslike as most business owners or team members would need to go back and think through the plan before jumping into a partnership. So my recommendation is to use the viewing to get as much information as possible about the property and the owner's position, to position your offer at a high level and to practise with a couple of soft closes. With that in mind I've put together a checklist of what to discuss at the viewing. This is also available as a download in the Online Resources (www.R2RGuide.com) so that you can easily print it and bring it with you on your next viewing.

- **Before the Viewing**

    ❏ Research comparable rental values for the property (what other similar houses are renting for in the area)

    ❏ Research the licensing and planning requirements for the area

    ❏ Research the potential room rental rates that you could receive from your tenants

❏ Search on Zoopla for any previous listings or floor plans for the property (Zoopla holds quite a bit of historical data for properties including old for rent and for sale adverts, purchase prices, rental values, etc.)

❏ What is the current EPC rating?

❏ What types of services (internet providers, utility providers, etc.) are available in the area?

❏ How much is the council tax?

❏ Estimate the maximum amount you can pay the owner

- **During the Viewing**

  ❏ Is the house currently tenanted?

    ❏ When are the current tenants leaving?

    ❏ Why are the current tenants leaving? OR

    ❏ How long has the house been empty?

    ❏ Why has it been empty?

  ❏ What furniture, if any, is included?

  ❏ What white goods, if any, are included?

  ❏ How old is the boiler? What type of boiler (combi, etc.?)

  ❏ Are the carpets/flooring in good condition?

  ❏ Do the walls need painting?

  ❏ What decoration, cleaning, refurb is the owner going to do before renting the property?

❏ Is the owner local? Are they involved in the management? (try to subtly understand as much as possible about the owner's situation)

❏ Are the windows double glazed?

❏ When was the last electrics certificate (**NICEIC** approved)?

❏ Are the smoke alarms interlinked?

❏ Is there a CO_2 detector?

❏ Are there any fire doors?

❏ Do all bedrooms have a safe fire exit (not through a high-risk/communal room)?

    ❏ Check windows open wide for rooms with doors leading to high-risk or communal rooms (so the tenants can escape safely through a window rather than through a high-risk room)

❏ Is there any sign of water damage, mould or condensation?

❏ Test the showers and taps for water pressure issues

❏ Measure bedroom and communal room sizes

❏ Is the garden easy to maintain?

❏ Is there parking?

❏ Where is the nearest bus stop?

❏ What type of construction is the property?

❏ Is the exterior (pointing, roof) in good repair?

❏ Is the house secure? Locks on doors/windows?

❏ Explain at a high level how you work (using information from the scripts in the previous section)

❏ Provide your one-pagers and marketing leaflets if the agent/owner has questions about how you work – see the Online Resources (www. R2RGuide.com) for examples

❏ Provide a business card for the agent/owner

❏ Ask for contact information for the lettings manager/key decision maker at the lettings agency

- **After the Viewing**

    ❏ Confirm the room sizes meet the required standards for the area

    ❏ Confirm the estimated rent you can receive from the tenants

    ❏ Recalculate the maximum amount you can offer the owner

    ❏ Write out your offer in an easy to follow manner and prepare to provide both a verbal and written offer

    ❏ Follow up regularly about the property and your offer

4.4 Presenting Your Offer

This is it – the big moment! It's time to present your offer to the owner/letting agent. This was a step in the last section (as part of the Viewing Checklist in 4.3) but now we are going to go into a bit more detail.

But first let's recap about how to build up to the offer and explain what you do. Here is a list of things you should already have provided to the agent/owner before you get to the offer stage:

- Professional website providing more information about how you work, ideally with a video and some testimonials or examples of some of your properties.

- One-pagers which are marketing pamphlets that explain in a bit more depth how you work. I've got examples in the Online Resources (www.R2RGuide. com) which include a Frequently Asked Questions (FAQs) page along with an About Us page.

- A draft copy of your contracts. Most people like to have a read through of the legals before they make any agreements. You can preface it by saying this is a generic copy and you can make some changes but don't make it sound like the sky is the limit and you can write it to suit them. Most businesses do not offer blank paper contracts to their customers. They have a standard contract that they use in most situations and that is what your agent/landlord is going to be expecting from you. We do have some contracts available and you can learn more in the Online Resources (www.R2RGuide.com).

- A ballpark figure or estimate of what you can generally pay for properties of that size. Keep it generic and reasonably wide. This is normally verbal but can be written in email if that is how you are communicating with the stakeholder. I normally provide this before doing the viewing so we can make sure we are in the same ballpark so that neither of us is wasting time. Be broad in this estimate as if your quote is too high and the property is a dump the owner/agent will be upset if your final offer is below your estimate (as no one thinks their property is that bad).

Once you've had a couple of high-level conversations, provided the above information and done a viewing, it's time for the final offer. I always expect negotiation from this point so DO NOT offer your highest amount first. I usually leave around £30-£50 wiggle room in my offers. Everyone likes to feel that they are getting a bargain and they have been able to negotiate you down. In the beginning I used to offer my best and final price right at the beginning because I hate haggling, but then I realised everyone else expects to be able to negotiate and wouldn't believe me when I said it was my best and final offer. So now I just round up and leave room for negotiating.

Then how do you present that offer? I always provide a written offer, normally via email. Then follow it up with a phone call to see if they have any questions. We try to phrase the offer in a Problem, Promise, Product, Proof, Purpose format. The email would normally go something like this (don't include the text in the [ ] – that is just for your information):

Dear Mr Jones

Thank you so much for the opportunity of viewing your property yesterday. It is perfectly suited for our clients based on its great location and generous room sizes and as such we would like to make a formal offer for a long-term lease.

[PROBLEM] I know you said you have been having problems with your recent tenants causing quite a bit of damage to the house. We have seen that a lot in student properties and this is what we love to help with.

[PROMISE] Our clients are all young professionals that work in the local area for companies such as BMW, British Gas and the other businesses at the business and science parks. We go through a detailed vetting process and are very hands-on in the management of the property so that only the best tenants get in and with our hands-on management style there is no chance of unruly tenants taking over. We treat your property like it was our own!

[PRODUCT] Our normal lease period is five years, which provides you with the certainty of knowing exactly how much rent you are getting each month. We also take over all of the non-structural maintenance so you can plan your life without worries of unexpected expenses.

As we mentioned during the viewing, we would need to do a bit of work to get it up to the standard expected by our clients, which we would do at our cost, thereby adding value to your property. And of course we keep it in this condition throughout our lease as this is how we keep our clients happy so you get the property back in the same or better condition as it is currently in.

Finally, we deal with all the tenant queries so that you never have to worry about a 2am phone call because a tenant locked themselves out again. We've got everything covered so that you can focus on the more important things in life.

We are excited to be able to offer you £1,500 per month for your property on 123 Church Street on our five-year commercial lease option.

[PROOF] We know we can deliver on our promise as we've got a lot of experience. You can see some of our recent property transformations on our website and we are happy to put you in contact with a couple of our current landlords so you can speak to them about their experience in working with us.

[PURPOSE] Once again, thank you for your time and giving us the opportunity to serve you. We are incredibly proud of our unique offering that allows you to have a completely hands-free, hassle-free and reliable property management experience.

I will follow up with you tomorrow with a phone call to see if you have any questions about our offer. I look forward to speaking with you again.

Kind regards

Jacquie

Please make sure you don't just copy and paste the above but put it in your own words so that you are comfortable and confident in repeating it verbally. When you call them the following day (I like to give them a day to let things sink in) you will want to say pretty much the same thing that you wrote in your email and you will need it to flow confidently. Make sure you cover the benefits that the landlord will get and how you will solve their problem. In my example the problem was that the landlord had students as his tenants and they were wrecking his house. I explained how we rent to young professionals who are carefully vetted and that we also maintain the property. So he doesn't need to worry about students or maintenance issues.

If you follow a similar format and cover similar points (tailored to your specific landlord situation) and use language you are comfortable with, you will have the makings of a great offer. And make sure you always follow up with them when you say you will. So if you say you'll call them at 2pm the following day, call them at 2pm, not 3pm or 2.30pm. Don't break promises before you even get started!

When you call be prepared for a bit of negotiating. Know your limits based on the numbers (Step 3.6) and make sure you don't go above what you can afford. If you feel pressured on the phone don't make a decision. You can always say that you have to get any changes approved by your supervisor. Then hang up, take a deep breath, refresh yourself with the numbers and your estimates and prepare a counter-offer for them. The key in negotiating is making sure you understand the owner's problem, because if you can clearly articulate how you are solving their problem (and they have a genuine problem that isn't solved by a normal tenancy or letting agent) then you should be able to do a deal. Ultimately, as a Rent to Rent business owner you are a property problem solver. You are responsible for solving your landlord's property problems with your Rent to Rent solution and need to be able to articulate clearly how you can help. All the tools in this book have led you up to this point and given you the background and tools you need to present your offer to the owner. Not every property is right for a Rent to Rent but the more offers you make, the more opportunities you have to grow your business.

STEP 5:
NEXT STEPS/SCALING

You made it! Well done on making it through the four steps for getting started in your Rent to Rent business. This last step is a bit of a bonus and prelude to the next book in the series: *Rent to Rent: Scaling for Growth* (expected in 2018).

You'll notice that we didn't cover in this book what to do when you get a Rent to Rent deal or managing tenants – that's because this is covered in my first book, *Rent to Rent: Your Questions Answered*. Like it sounds, that book is a Q&A style book and will answer all your practical questions about actually running and managing your Rent to Rent properties. This book takes you up to the point where your business is set up and you can go out and find the deals. While I wrote them a bit out of order, here is the sequence for the books that you can use for more information:

Rent to Rent: Getting Started Guide – First four steps taking you through the set up of your Rent to Rent business:

1. Plan Your Business

2. Set Up Your Business

3. Research Your Area

4. Do a Lot of Viewings

Rent to Rent: Your Questions Answered – Has five major sections covering all areas of a Rent to Rent business answering the most frequently asked questions about Rent to Rent. It covers a bit of the information in the *Getting Started Guide* and then takes it further through managing the properties and tenants:

1. Rent to Rent Basics

2. Choosing Your Area

3. Finding Rent to Rent Deals

4. Managing a Light Refurb

5. Tenants

Rent to Rent: Scaling for Growth – Is the final book in the series and is expected in 2018. This will be ideal for people that have two or three Rent to Rent properties and are looking to start to set up their systems so they can easily scale and grow the company by bringing on a team and putting processes in place.

While my books and the Online Resources (www. R2RGuide.com) are great to give you an overview on the Rent to Rent business, this may not be enough for everyone. Some people will be able to read these books and have all the information they need to get their business up and running while others may need some more information and support.

If you have never run your own business before or have absolutely no experience in property it may be advisable for you to undertake some additional education because, after all, most of us needed training for our current careers. I spent four years at university studying accounting before I started my original accounting job. And while you don't need a university degree to start your Rent to Rent business, if you have no experience (in business or in property) this is a good opportunity to learn as much as possible now before you get stuck with a technical detail in your Rent to Rent business and people's lives are impacted (tenants or landlords).

In the rest of this section I'll go through some other places that you can go to get more information on Rent to Rent and quickly building your Rent to Rent business.

5.1 Online Resources

I have talked about the Online Resources throughout the book. I set these up as a key addition to this book to give you even more information to help you get your Rent to Rent business up and running. This is like a mini membership site and training course all in one – and it's completely included in the price you paid for this book! So there are no additional fees for you to access the additional tools included there.

I've recorded videos, added checklists, guides, articles, links to my favourite resources and suppliers and much, much more so that you can easily leverage what I've done to get started quickly in your own business.

You can see all the resources at: www.R2RGuide.com

5.2 Courses and Further Training

There are many courses available on Rent to Rent and property investing. Some are better than others. If you are part of any of the online property communities, you will likely have seen long tirades against courses and training providers. I am going to disagree with all the course haters out there as I strongly believe in getting educated and that we are all constantly on a journey of continuing education.

It is very important that you understand who your trainer is and what their background is before jumping in and paying thousands of pounds for a training course – and of course never ever joint venture with someone that you don't trust and have not done your due diligence on. But there is definitely a place for additional education – be that in person or online.

Most trainers and people running courses will have a couple of different levels available so you can try them out at their cheapest introductory course. This will help you to ensure that you like their teaching style and their ethics before you jump into the longer and more expensive courses.

As a word of caution, there is the possibility of course overload as well. You DO NOT need to do every training course out there, especially if you have read my books and used the Online Resources (www.R2RGuide.com) available with this book. It is very important that you set a budget for your ongoing training needs. You may not have the money to invest in additional courses right now – and that's OK. You've got the information you need to get started and if you have more time than money there is plenty of free information available on the internet (just make sure you are using a reliable source). If you don't have time to trawl the internet and put together the material yourself then definitely consider further training. And everyone should have an ongoing budget set up for continuing education.

My personal journey has included around £100,000 of education since I stopped being an accountant and started my property business. I chose Simon Zutshi as my property mentor and started with his three-day Mastermind Accelerator Course and then went on to his 12-month Mastermind Programme, where I finished in the top five. Since then I've been focusing on the business side of things and have been working with a number of mentors, the main one is Roger Hamilton who wrote the foreword of this book. He is one of the leaders of the entrepreneur movement and is helping entrepreneurs around the world to grow purposeful and passion-filled businesses. And I've done a number of other courses with other trainers. I'll provide more information on my favourites in the Online Resources (www.R2RGuide.com) so that you can check them out when you are ready.

I also offer a number of training courses from a general Introduction to Rent to Rent Course through to a nine-week Rent to Rent Mastery Programme. There is something for everyone including a number of specific small courses focused on detailed topics like setting up your referencing process. You can see all of my courses and training at the Rent to Rent Academy Website: www.RenttoRentAcademy.co.uk.

So if you don't have the funds right now for more training and courses, don't worry. You don't need any more. You can get started with the information you have available to you in my books and for free online. But please make sure you add ongoing training into your budget for when you start bringing in the cash flow as if you want to continue to grow your business, you need to also grow yourself.

5.3 Community and Membership

If you are looking to stay in touch with the latest in Rent to Rent and connect with a vibrant community of Rent to Renters across the UK, then I highly recommend that you check out my membership options. These are different from courses in that they are ongoing for as long as you want to stay involved and more information will be added regularly along with monthly calls connecting you with other Rent to Renters and their stories.

An ongoing membership is perfect for people who understand what they need to do in their business but don't want to feel like they are doing it alone. They want to have a supportive and confidential place to go to ask questions and hear others people's stories and experiences. And they want to stay up to date on the latest ideas and strategies in Rent to Rent. The world is constantly changing, especially with changing legislation, and an ongoing membership will help you to always stay current and a step ahead of the competition.

I've got couple of levels of membership available if you are interested in an ongoing community and information that is constantly being updated. The best place to go for more information is www.RenttoRentAcademy.co.uk.

5.4 Mentoring/Coaching

Mentoring and Coaching is a great opportunity for bespoke one to one help that is tailored specifically to you and your needs. This is perfect if you are struggling with a specific area and need to dig a bit deeper to help you move to the next level in your business. Again, like with courses and training, there are a lot of different providers out there and it is very important to find someone that you trust and who has similar values and ethics as you and someone who has been there and done it. Most coaches and mentors will offer introductory sessions for you to get to know each other to make sure both parties want to work together.

I offer one to one coaching and mentoring as well – although my time has become extremely limited so I only work with a select number of people on a one to one basis and this is on application only. If you are interested in working further with me, the best way is through my membership programme as I offer monthly calls and group mentoring there. I also offer FREE 10-minute calls so we can have a chat on where you are at and see what next step is right for you. You can schedule the **FREE** 10-minute call here http://R2R.property/10min.

If you check the Online Resources (www.R2RGuide.com) there is more information on coaching and mentoring if you are looking to choose someone to work with you one to one on your journey.

5.6 Final Words

Thank you so much for letting me join with you on your journey in Rent to Rent! I really enjoy being able to give back and help others to create their financial freedom and live the lives of their dreams. I truly believe that we all have such an amazing opportunity right now – an opportunity that wasn't available previously because this is the age of the entrepreneur. We are able to build our lives to suit our lifestyles. I don't think anyone should have to work in a 9-5 job that they hate because they feel trapped and worried that there is nothing else out there for them. I am passionate in my belief that we all have the same opportunities to create lives that we love and am focused on helping to promote that as much as I can. And I love hearing all the success stories of people that have been able to change their lives, to spend more time with family and with the important things in life. NOW is the time to start living!

The last thought I want to leave you with is yes – you can do it! It takes time, you won't build your business overnight, and no matter how many 'overnight' success stories you hear, none of them truly happened in an instant. Companies like AirBnB and Uber were years in the making before they became billion dollar unicorns. We often don't see the struggles of others and only see the success. And you will have struggles, some days will be harder than others but you can succeed if you stay focused and keep moving forward. One day at a time, one step before the next. Take action and build the life of your dreams!

> *A dream written down with a date becomes a goal.*
>
> *A goal broken down into steps becomes a plan.*
>
> *A plan backed by action makes your dreams come true.*

Greg S. Reid

ABOUT THE AUTHOR

Jacquie Edwards started out just like everyone else working a 9-5 job in someone else's office. She knew there must be something better to life but didn't know what to do about it. She realised that she was trading her time for money and that this would only get her so far, and she needed to find financial freedom in order to live the life she deserved.

In 12 months Jacquie was able to build a Rent to Rent business with a recurring income of over £100,000 from properties she didn't own and subsequently published her first book, *Rent to Rent: Your Questions Answered* to help others achieve the same results.

Since her last book Jacquie has continued to build her Rent to Rent business and now has over 100 tenants in 20 HMOs which has doubled her income. With a strong team in place she is now able to work from anywhere and has even more time to help others become financially free!

If you would like to accelerate your investing and work with Jacquie, please check out her website at http://R2R. property/10min to schedule a FREE starter call. Times are limited so act quickly!

Printed in Great Britain
by Amazon